About Island Press

Since 1984, the nonprofit organization Island Press has been stimulating, shaping, and communicating ideas that are essential for solving environmental problems worldwide. With more than 1,000 titles in print and some 30 new releases each year, we are the nation's leading publisher on environmental issues. We identify innovative thinkers and emerging trends in the environmental field. We work with world-renowned experts and authors to develop cross-disciplinary solutions to environmental challenges.

Island Press designs and executes educational campaigns, in conjunction with our authors, to communicate their critical messages in print, in person, and online using the latest technologies, innovative programs, and the media. Our goal is to reach targeted audiences—scientists, policy makers, environmental advocates, urban planners, the media, and concerned citizens—with information that can be used to create the framework for long-term ecological health and human well-being.

Island Press gratefully acknowledges major support from The Bobolink Foundation, Caldera Foundation, The Curtis and Edith Munson Foundation, The Forrest C. and Frances H. Lattner Foundation, The JPB Foundation, The Kresge Foundation, The Summit Charitable Foundation, Inc., and many other generous organizations and individuals.

The opinions expressed in this book are those of the author(s) and do not necessarily reflect the views of our supporters.

The Intergalactic Design Guide

The
Intergalactic
Design Guide

Harnessing
the Creative
Potential of
Social Design

Cheryl Heller

◐ **ISLAND**PRESS | Washington | Covelo | London

Library of Congress Control Number: 2018947148

All Island Press books are printed on environmentally responsible materials.

Manufactured in the United States of America
10 9 8 7 6 5 4 3 2 1

Keywords: Aquafil, BRCK, Brown's Super Stores, Buffalo Niagara Medical Center, Butaro District Hospital, climate change, collaboration, communication, context, creativity, critical thinking, culture, *Design for the Other 90%*, design thinking, Erik Hersman, experiential learning, food waste, GHESKIO Cholera Treatment Center, human capacity, human-centered design, identity, Interface, invention, impact design, Jeffrey Brown, Josh Treuhaft, Kenyan elections, leadership, MASS Design Group, Matt Enstice, Michael Murphy, MutualCity, networking, Paul Polak, participation, partnership, poverty, prototype, Rachel Brown, Ray Anderson, recycling, resilience, Ruth Gates, Salvage Supperclub, Sisi ni Amani, social innovation design, Spring Health, Uplift, vision

FOR GARY

As *Homo sapiens's* entry in any intergalactic design competition, industrial civilization would be tossed out at the qualifying round. It doesn't fit. It won't last. The scale is wrong. And even its apologists admit that it is not very pretty. The design failures of industrially/technologically driven societies are manifest in the loss of diversity of all kinds, destabilization of the earth's biogeochemical cycles, pollution, soil erosion, ugliness, poverty, injustice, social decay, and economic instability.

DAVID ORR,
Earth in Mind

Mrs. Cavendish wanted it all
to mean something in a world crazed
and splattered with the gook
of apparent significance, and meaning
had an affinity for being elsewhere.

STEPHEN DUNN,
"Mrs. Cavendish and the Dancer"

Contents

Preface

THIS BOOK IS THE SYNTHESIS OF MANY YEARS OF PRACTICE, observation, and explanation. I have been a practicing designer during the profession's most dramatic changes, from the introduction of the technologies that changed its very nature through designers' awakening to the power they have to create social good as well as empty consumption. My clients have included leading multinational corporations in almost every industry, entrepreneurs of all kinds, foundations, nonprofits, and global nongovernmental organizations working to save the planet and end human inequity. I have made the journey from a lone "creative," whose job was to produce exciting new ideas on demand, to an agent of change who facilitates others in developing ideas for themselves. I have learned from—and, I hope, provided value to—each of them.

Over all these contexts and experiences, I have observed what works in the short term and over time. I have studied how successful people succeed, how the disruptors disrupt, and what, across gulfs of culture, size, and vision, they have in common. From Paul Polak, with his astounding work to create new economies that end poverty, to Erik Hersman, whose serial technological innovations have touched, and connected, many millions of people, to the organizers of the 1975 women's strike in Iceland, who won gender equality for their country, the methods for designing change are essentially the same.

Explanation is making sense of what's been learned and observed. It is inviting everyone in and making this new way of approaching change accessible. Explanation is both the hardest and the most interesting part. For me, it has included developing and chairing the first master of fine arts program in social design, a nine-year process (so far) of translating the practice of social design into experiential learning that sends graduates out into the world to lead their own change for good. And, of course, it includes the transformational two-and-a-half-year process of writing this book.

Three things urgently need to be explained. First, social design is the best method we have to create a viable future for our civilization because it transforms us as it changes the things around us. There are examples of its effectiveness in action everywhere; there is no need to delay getting started. Second, while brilliant innovators do it instinctively, each gravitating to common principles and processes, social design is something that, with practice and dedication, everyone who wants to can learn. And, finally, we need to learn it now. As the Chinese proverb advises, if we don't change our direction, we're likely to end up where we're going.

It is my humble hope that this book will inspire more leaders, like the ones included here, to find the social designer in themselves. And that it will inspire confidence in those already doing so, by confirming for them that they're on the right path. What we urgently need is for new generations of leaders to step forward and put these principles for mutuality and resilience into practice. Please, do. And thank you.

—*Cheryl Heller*

CHAPTER 1

The Answer
to Everything

A BICYCLE SALESMAN ON TENTH AVENUE AND FIFTY-EIGHTH STREET in Manhattan offers practical wisdom to customers who walk into the store to buy their first serious bike. His body speaks with road-tested authority before he does, with quadriceps the size of footballs and calves that look as if they were blown up with a bicycle pump. Tutorials include demos on changing flats, adjusting seats, working gears on tricky hills, and getting out of toe clips in time to avoid toppling sideways toward the pavement, bike in hand.

"I'll give you one more piece of advice," he says. "You're going to be inclined to stare at the pothole or the curb or open cab door when you're out on the streets, thinking that's the best way not to hit it. Don't. Look at the space beside it, no matter how narrow. Because what you look at is where you'll go."

Somewhat more eloquently, the philosopher William Irwin Thompson said that, like fly-fishers, "we cast images in front of ourselves and then slowly reel ourselves into them, turning them into reality." The point is pretty much the same whether you're riding a bike, catching a fish, or trying to imagine a future for humankind.

But it's the concreteness of the bike salesman's wisdom that makes it brilliant, the specificity of it that connects our pothole-level reality with the loftiest universal ideals.

Instead of staring into the dismal picture put out by twenty-four-hour-a-day media and entertainment, trapping ourselves in an endless inventory of what's wrong, can we picture the reality we want to see? That vision would be of a civilization with its best years still in the future: a world in which everyone who wants useful work has it and more than a handful of people have money and power, a world where industries aren't fighting over the remnants of extracted resources and we don't poison ourselves with toxic chemicals. Where we live in a state of mutuality with each other and with nature, not a frenzied destruction of her. Where the reasons to trust outweigh the need to protect.

This is not Oz I'm describing, or a naive vision of utopia, or blindness to the difficulties inherent in maintaining a species as ubiquitous, acquisitive, self-centered, and frequently violent as our own, but a vision that accepts our inherent character and channels its collective creativity in mostly benign, productive ways.

It's a civilization that would have a shot at first prize in any intergalactic design competition.

Unlike the traditional design processes that have formed so much of our modern society, social design is a methodology for changing the human condition. Not changing the world, as so many like to say, because the world itself is not in need of change. Social design is a system, first and foremost, for designing fundamental changes in ourselves: a shift in who we think we are, how we perceive and treat each other, what we believe is possible and can work together to create. It instills a belief in human agency and creativity and builds the capacity for communities to reimagine new stories and new realities for themselves.

"Social design" is a term that entered the lexicon around 2006. The name can be interpreted literally as the design (or redesign) of societies, at either ultralocal or large scales. It incorporates both the physical and the intangible, the human relationships that create communities and form societies.

Within the army of people already working to address social issues of poverty, equity, and their kin, the question inevitably arises (with varying degrees of suspicion) as to how social design is different from what they already do, and exactly what, at a pothole-specific level, it is.

Design has always been in service to what's next and, sometimes, to what is really needed. Social design is, in one way, simply design's evolutionary trajectory in relation to the effects of technology. Yet it is revolutionary. Almost nothing about it is new except its organization into a system and its application to human relationships instead of only artifacts. Yet that has never been done before. It's a particular combination of activities performed in a certain order, informed by a set of principles, and mastered through a combination of hard and soft skills. Yet it turns the established ways of working upside down.

There is nothing magical about it, although some like to make it seem that way. All those willing to invest themselves fully can learn to do it, and while much of it seems like logic too simple to merit study, significant rigor, discipline, and time are required to do it well. It doesn't guarantee success, but it does increase the odds of making things work for more people instead of only a few. Most of all, it changes anyone who practices it: social design puts us in touch with our own creativity, resourcefulness, and purpose.

Unlike designing with physical resources, social design is often intangible, disappearing into the evidence it produces—the polar opposite of making a fancy new car or phone, where there's a solid artifact for all to judge or admire. Yet the invisible forces that are the materials of social design control the way we think, the things we make, the way we act, and whether or not we'll succeed in finding a viable way to live and work together.

Nearly a quarter century ago, David Orr wrote *Earth in Mind*[1] and called us out on the shoddy design of our industrial civilization. It's an understatement to say that for now, the situation has not improved. Not for lack of awareness, though, since the evidence is everywhere.

The drinking water in Flint, Michigan, poisons the city's residents. The air quality in Beijing poisons citizens there. Five hundred children under the age of five die every day in India from issues of contaminated water and poor sanitation. Babies are born with opioid addiction, costing billions of dollars in health care. Two out of three adults in the United States are either grossly overweight or obese, and the richest 1 percent are wealthier than the "bottom" 90 percent combined. Terrorists drive onto sidewalks in an effort to kill pedestrians. The Amazon jungle is being destroyed at the rate of one and one-half acres per second, and half of all the 22-million-year-old coral reefs on the planet have died in the past 30 years because of climate change. Without radical modification, our current trajectory leads only to disaster—death by the fallout from climate change, epidemic, or nuclear war, each resulting in one way or another from the unsustainable civilization we have built.

We do not suffer, though, from a scarcity of ideas for how to remedy our plight. In *Blessed Unrest*, Paul Hawken called the widespread awakening of social and environmental activism the "greatest movement on earth."[2] It includes small grassroots efforts everywhere and massive global programs and technologies with the power and scale to transform life as we know it. Inventors have developed renewable sources of energy, and entrepreneurs grow materials from mushrooms that replace those made from plastic.[3] Financial inclusion services have been developed that make it possible for people without money to join the global economy. Dozens of designs for cookstoves don't suffocate the people who use them; fishing nets exist that do not trap and kill hundreds of thousands of loggerhead and leatherback sea turtles and seabirds every year. People everywhere are either working to raise awareness about the things that need addressing or fixing current problems and developing new technologies to circumvent them. The list is endless, and tallying it would be akin to trying to count the number of restaurants in New York City while new ones close and open every day.

This book offers a practitioner's perspective on social design, not a technical, academic, or theoretical one. There are books on design research methods, history, heroes, and contributions. There are beautiful books on the craft of design, its materials and aesthetics. Here, no attempt has been made to include everything there is to know, only enough—and, I hope, plenty—for everyone who wants to practice social design to understand how and where it works. And to see that the only place to begin is where they are.

The examples included are about practitioners, people who learn from doing and act their way to change. They set out, driven by an audacious purpose, but often with no advance plan for how to accomplish it. They make decisions based on evidence, navigating in uncertainty, moving forward one step at a time. Yet they accomplish the improbable, upending accepted notions of "how things are done." Who would expect, for example, that a global business could be built by selling to people who make less than two dollars per day? Or that a grassroots movement could use text messages to curtail violence among people who were fired up to fight? Or that scientists and hotel companies could collaborate to save coral reefs? These are some of the challenges that social designers are taking on.

The social designers included here are remarkable people, not just because they have experience, special skills, and intelligence, but because they are leaders. They are the people who step up, who decide to act instead of only thinking about it, and who engage wildly diverse collaborators in the process, leaving the comfort of their silos of expertise to continually learn and grow. Their stories illustrate how others, compelled by their values and driven to make their work matter, can do the same.

By any of the names used to describe it, including "human-centered design," "impact design," and "social innovation design," social design is gaining traction in expected as well as surprising places far beyond the stories told here. Global corporations use it to ignite creativity and engagement within their cultures; foundations embed it into their efforts to end poverty and improve human health. Institutions in the acronym community, such as the UN, UNICEF, USAID, and DFID,[4] use social design to develop new approaches, erase the boundaries of internal silos, and step around archaic bureaucratic processes. It is used to address crime and homelessness in neighborhoods, to revitalize America's Rust Belt cities, to jump-start economies in India, to connect hundreds of thousands of women to prenatal and infant care across Africa. It is a system that is relevant to any human endeavor.

Each of the stories on the pages that follow opens a window into a future different from the one we see in the news every day. All offer proof that it's possible to change the direction in which we're headed, and all illustrate the process for getting there. Unlike the solitary heroes of the past who decided what was best for everyone else, these collaborative leaders engage everyone they touch. Paul Polak creates new markets and industries where they didn't exist before. He helps people earn their way out of poverty by asking them why they're poor and then doing "the simple and obvious" to help them change it. At eighty-four, he is launching three new enterprises with the potential to reach 20 million more of the roughly 70 percent of the people in the world who earn less than two dollars per day.

Michael Murphy has built a global architecture practice by eschewing the traditional priorities of his industry, hacking what others accept as an inviolate set of rules as to how, and for whom, built environments are created, and by involving the communities where he builds in the plans. He is reimagining the scope and purpose of architectural design and, in the process, redefining what it means to be an architect. Ruth Gates is prodding academia into action and building a network of unusual collaborators to save the ocean's coral reefs by scaling the resilient "supercorals" she's breeding. Rachel Brown reduced violence in Kenya by activating a massive grassroots movement of peace builders, using text messages to infiltrate communities with the information they needed to understand the issues. She is now practicing her methods of defusing hate speech and spreading peace in other parts of the world.

Jeffrey Brown has built a grocery store empire in the poorest neighborhoods of Philadelphia by asking communities what will work for them. He staffs his business with enthusiastic local team members, almost one-third of whom used to be in jail. In Buffalo, New York, the Buffalo Niagara Medical Campus has changed the city's image of itself and changed its fortunes, igniting new energy and growth through a networked, collaborative approach to creativity. Erik Hersman builds connectivity to bring education and opportunity to Africa's frontier markets, creating what he hopes will become the continent's first billion-dollar homegrown enterprise. And Interface, a carpet manufacturer based in Atlanta, Georgia, is engaging residents of remote fishing villages, using its supply chain to save precious human and marine ecosystems while maintaining Interface's position as the largest carpet tile company in the world.

Unbeknownst to these leaders, they all follow the same principles and use the essential social design process. Every one of them has turned the conventional processes and fixed opinions of their industries on their heads. They have demonstrated the vision and courage to see, and then act on, instincts counter to what they were taught and told. These are principles and methods applicable to any endeavor that relies on human beings acting in collaboration.

It is not an accident that only two of the projects here are led by people who call themselves designers. Some of the best and most effective exemplars of social design don't apply that label to themselves. They are not designers in the way the term has traditionally been defined.

Because social design is based on creating *with* others and not *for* them, the old, calcified distinctions between designers and nondesigners don't count. Social design does not suffer bystanders. It depends on the collective cocreation of a future, and it succeeds when all participants feel ownership of the process. The answer to everything is to stop trying to change everything, to focus instead on transforming ourselves. These leaders exemplify how it's done.

HOW IT APPLIES TO YOU

The experience of social design is transformative. It shifts our focus away from searching for solutions in something or someone outside ourselves or searching for the "right" decision that will change things. It builds capacity within participants for resourcefulness and an ability to act on the basis of what is happening rather than what was assumed in advance. It puts everyone in the middle, as protagonists, collaborators, and mediators, instead of on the outside. It forms a collective sense of self that requires people to look more deeply into their own community and place, whether that's a global corporate culture, a rural village of two hundred people, or an urban center of multiple millions. It allows us to see what is unique about every instance and place, as well as the common needs that make us the same. It is a way to hear our own voices in context with the voices of others who are never heard. This is the transformative power of social design to change us, so that we can apply these mutualistic principles everywhere throughout our lives. The same principles that apply to urban food deserts, coral reefs, hospitals, and violence prevention apply everywhere, to everyone.

CAUTIONS

Common sense is not the same as wisdom. A familiar expression in the systems thinking world is that "every system is perfectly designed to produce the results it produces." In other words, the only way to alter an outcome is to change the system that determines it. Applied to modern culture, this means that the system we've designed will continue to produce outcomes we don't want unless we redesign it. In order to move from helplessly watching what's happening to changing it, we must be able to see, understand, and intervene in the invisible dynamics that drive our behavior.

What systems lie behind our addiction to acquisitions? What prevents us from curtailing our destructive habits? Why do we passively accept unspoken "rules" about what is sensible or right or kosher that we know aren't right when we stop to think about them? When we do see ourselves clearly, why don't we change? Why does our species seem incapable of acting together in our own best interest? Plenty of research has been conducted to investigate these questions. Theories range from the belief that a flaw in our brains prevents us from comprehending dangers in the future, to the fact that since ours is the most violent species ever to walk the planet (the reason we survived), it is therefore simply our nature to continually war with each other and wipe out any creatures we view as competition.

What we accept as common sense is narcotic, a hegemony of shared practices and beliefs we never question because they're all we've known. "Common sense" in business can take the form of blind faith in the predictive power of a carefully written five-year plan. Or it can mean succumbing to the placebo effect of adding committees and departments as a way to solve problems that no committee or department could hope to solve, because the problems are endemic to the organization itself. Outside the workplace, so-called common sense supports our habit of discarding current devices every time a new model is introduced or putting chemicals on our lawns and into the water supply because we want to be seen as responsible homeowners.

Wisdom, on the other hand, is full awareness—in and of the moment. It is judgment applied to sound action, rather than preprogrammed motives and responses. Wisdom is indigenous—to our senses, to our physical being, and to the places where we live. It is personal, individual, earned through experience over a lifetime. Yet we find it easier to substitute herdlike "common sense" for wisdom. We drown wisdom out every day with billions of sound bites from news, advertising, and social media. We clear-cut it and smother it under shopping malls and high-rises, parking lots and apps. The time has come to disinter it, dust it off, and reexamine it in the light of our present circumstances. The social design process is a way to begin.

Like the bicycle salesman's warning to pay attention to where we want to go, much of the process of social design may sound like common sense, a been-there-done-that kind of déjà vu. In practice, though, it feels altogether new. Aquafil, Interface's supplier of recycled materials, discovered that European Union regulations allow for shipping discarded materials out of the EU to unseen countries but not shipping the world's trash back in. Regulations that seem like common sense can prove to be unwise.

Social design requires a kind of ignorance, a state of mind some call "not knowing": a willingness to reconsider things we thought we knew, to avoid making fast conclusions based on superficial assessment. It discounts the very things that have been rewarded inside corporations: the ability to be decisive, be the smartest person in the room. Generations before our own had more opportunity to discover, had things to learn that no one within reach of an algorithm knew. It's harder, in the twenty-first century, to find the unknown, to maintain curiosity, when too much information is always available.

LANGUAGE CAN CLARIFY OR CONFUSE, INCLUDE OR EXCLUDE

Every attempt has been made to strip this book of linguistic crimes: jargon, argot, inside baseball, and the false gods of shortcuts and easy fixes. Certain popular labels have intentionally been omitted. Design thinking has gained popularity in business, social organizations, and education. It is a trope that substitutes for a more comprehensive process, a brainstorming template tied to an approach that delights people new to the creative process, helping to open their thinking and consider their users' point of view. When used out of context, it lacks rigor, standards, and metrics.

"Design" and "thinking" are two conjoined words that have become, in prevalence and purview, symptomatic of the confusing language to which all new fields fall prey. "Design thinking" has, in common with "impact investing," tautology posing as revelation. All design involves thinking, whether good or poor, and all investment has impact of one kind or another. Yet, in both cases, entire industries have emerged in service to these vagaries. The problem in the case of design is that it legitimizes the notion that the creative process can be reduced to a set of rote, daylong or even hour-long exercises with sticky notes. In the case of investing, it implies there is an alternative, acceptable kind of investment that excludes responsibility for its impact. Both expressions lend exceptional status to values that should be part of the norm, allowing people to believe they are solving systemic problems by being a little bit creative or somewhat responsible.

EVERYTHING HAS A BACK AND A FRONT
Knowledge of how to intervene in the lives of others is not a license to do so. Mastery of the tools does not include permission to use them thoughtlessly or with the arrogance that privileged people have for so many decades shown. The social design process, at its best, erases otherness, instills humility, and permeates the silos of expertise. It is not to be taken lightly or used part-time.

THIS IS A MOMENT IN TIME
Social design is a work in process. Anything we do, or try to capture, is fluid and can reflect only what we know now. The cases included here are all in process; some are still launching, some are in transition, and some are hitting one of the many inflection points they will encounter along the way. They will continue to evolve, as will our understanding and evaluation of social design—like culture itself, forever unfolding over time.

On the intergalactic part: If creatures from another planet ever talk one day about the fate of humans on Earth, the conversation won't be about how ergonomically our chairs were designed, how fashionable our clothes were, how erudite our theories, how much money we made, or how many industries were disrupted by design. They will say either that we pulled ourselves out of a near-fatal collision at the last possible second, or that we missed the greatest opportunity ever handed to any species in the infinite cosmos and blew up the sweetest planet that ever was.

The contention of this book is that it's all a question of design.

CHAPTER 2

Seeing Edges and Patterns, Scoping and Framing

SOCIAL DESIGN IS THE DESIGN OF RELATIONSHIPS, the creation of new social conditions intended to increase agency, health, creativity, equity, social justice, resilience, and connection to nature.

In cities, corporations, or any type of community, if the culture is a creative one, innovative ideas are continually generated there. In a culture aligned by just social values, those values drive actions over time. In a culture in which people have a sense of agency and possibility, possibilities are repeatedly found. These attributes become the norm. It is the inverse of a culture in which only certain people or departments are viewed as innovative, only those at the top dictate social values, and people expect that isolated events or interventions will lead to lasting change. Social design aims to create the cultural conditions in which the things you want to happen, happen more easily.

In his early work as a psychiatric researcher, looking outside the hospital walls for the causes of mental illness, Paul Polak called what he found "social architecture": the invisible social environment that, in this instance, caused only certain people with mental illnesses to have breakdowns and be hospitalized. That's a useful way to think about social design as well—as a kind of architectural practice that reimagines and reengineers an existing social structure to be more resilient and just, more conducive to keeping those living within it healthy.

When applied to specific issues and places, desired outcomes can be defined with precision, concretely and fully. Polak determines the impact he wants to incite in great detail, in financial as well as human terms. He wants to create consistent access to, and a desire for, clean water in rural Indian villages so that businesses launched there will grow sustainably on their own. Marine biologist Ruth Gates has envisioned how a network of diverse collaborators, from different parts of the world, will define common values that drive the necessary actions to preserve coral reefs. Michael Murphy defines the outcomes for his built environments as creating more healthy cultures within and around them, inspiring healthier behavior in everyone involved. What makes social design universal is humans' common need for social justice and for human and environmental health. Within that, the possibilities for how to create the conditions to deliver on those needs are limitless.

At one time, design was defined as "intentionally rearranging resources,"[1] first physical ones and then also digital bits and bytes. Yet the "materials" of social design are not limited to physical or digital forms. They are human relationships and interactions as well. What makes social design different, in addition to the inclusion of human relationships, is that social design always has a higher social purpose. It is incited by a desire for greater good that drives all action in support of it. That means whatever products are developed in the process are part of a larger system or strategy. They are not the end goal, only the means by which the larger objective of a new outcome is reached. In the case of Gates, a "product" of her work is a new species of coral, for which she is rearranging genomes. But she is not creating a new coral for its own sake or to sell as a curiosity for aquariums. It is part of a larger strategy to create a system of scientists, industries, conservationists, and citizens who will use it to save coral reefs.

The skills required for social design are a tool kit of sorts, similar to the kind a very good carpenter might carry, filled with some favorite old implements with worn handles and patinas and some new tools that are shiny and sharp. A number of these skills have been part of the designer's art forever, such as synthesizing complex information and making it accessible; visualizing data and invisible systems so that insights and revelations and connections are available to everyone; reframing problems and questions to uncover root causes instead of symptoms; using abductive reasoning and sideways creative thinking; giving ideas physical form or representation and making them desirable—engaging and delighting people with the beauty or functionality of whatever has been created.

Other parts of social design have been incorporated from neighboring fields: the notion of "human-centered" design evolved from the "user-centered" shift in technology development, when a user's experience with products and services became the driving force for their design. And the idea that the best solutions are emergent rather than predicted or controlled—the use of prototypes and observation of people's responses as a way to iterate solutions instead of an "answer" decided upon in advance and force-fitted—comes from the study of living systems, the way nature works to "test" new ideas. It's the same insight that led to the Lean Startup methodology for entrepreneurs, which is slowly replacing our reliance on traditional five-year business plans.[2]

One challenge in describing social design, or in fact in introducing anything new into our overcrowded modern brains, is that the words available to us have lost their teeth. They've been co-opted, worn out, and shortened to sound bites so that they no longer have enough specificity to be meaningful. "Innovation," "impact," even "design," in some contexts, have been used to describe activities and outcomes that don't deserve to be called innovative, impactful, or intentionally designed. There is no solution for this except to be rigorous in the way we use words and to make sure we mean, and do, what we say. Recklessly throwing around the argot of social design without delivering on it earns membership only in a club to which there is little value in belonging. Stuffing "empathy" and "cocreation" or "collaboration" into sentences wherever room can be made proves naïveté, not mastery.

No one is served if words are canonized or overused. Empathy is sometimes treated like a rarefied skill requiring special instruction to learn, like cross-country skiing with rifles or turning out a perfect soufflé. In fact, except in sociopaths, empathy is a universal human instinct that occurs naturally. We just have to stop our own persistent internal chatter long enough to pay close, nonjudging attention to someone else. Put more simply, it happens every time we listen to another person (or another species) with an open mind. This does not mean distorting reason with unchecked emotion. It simply means learning to listen, which comes from nothing more than time and practice at seeing and feeling things from a perspective other than our own.

Similarly, "collaboration" and "cocreation" are often overused and can signal trendiness instead of rigor. The infatuation with brainstorming sessions has often made them a "cheap" substitute for a deeper, more disciplined approach. Brainstorming or "ideating" is decidedly more difficult to do successfully than to say, since it takes preparation and

The Objectives and Inquiry of Traditional and Social Design

TRADITIONAL APPROACH	SOCIAL DESIGN APPROACH

I have an idea.
I need to solve a problem.
I need to come up with the next killer product/service/innovation/
    strategy.
	I want to create a future condition in which . . .
	    our culture is fully engaged.
	    people understand the importance of healthy food and have access to it.

What do we have?
What do we need?
How will we do it?
What will it cost?
When can we have it?
	Who needs to participate?
	What is the context or system?
	How can we cocreate?
	What products or innovations
	    will we need?
	How can we prototype, iterate,
	    and learn?

strategy to develop a thoughtful, informed, and iterative creative process. It is also a fallacy that prioritizing cocreation means that nothing can happen unless a committee is present and everyone is involved in every conversation. Or that ideas aren't valid unless they're open-source. Within the many conversations and exchanges of ideas in the social design process, there is ample time and space, in fact a need, for the brilliance of individual minds as well as the power of the collective.

Recent research makes the case that groupthink is actually not as effective as individuals creating on their own.[3] It is certainly not the panacea that some of its promoters have made it out to be. It turns out that creativity happens most reliably, and most acutely, in isolation. Relatedly, it is generally true that the most creative people are introverts. The opportunity in social design is to find a way to incorporate the best of all personalities and ways of thinking.

There is a rhythm to creation and collaboration—coming together, iterating, going away, using silence and solitude. Insensitivity to these natural rhythms is counterproductive and frustrating. Some people aren't comfortable in "white space," when they don't yet have a solution. Discomfited participants in group work sessions who always need to know the next step can disrupt progress.

WHAT SOCIAL DESIGN IS NOT

Social design is not charity, which is giving money in the form of a donation. Nor is it cause marketing, which connects a corporate brand to a cause for the benefit of both the charity and the company's sales. It's not corporate social responsibility, which is a for-profit enterprise's efforts to behave responsibly toward the communities in which it works. Social design begins with a set of questions different from these traditional approaches to social change and design.

Traditional design is propelled by the need to develop a product or service that solves a problem or leads to financial gain. Social design begins with a higher purpose that transcends commerce. The process and the questions asked along the way are not the same.

CHAPTER 3

Past as Prologue

UNLIKE ART, which by definition is free of commercial agenda, design has served as a powerful tool for business since the dawn of the industrial age. It has built global brands, disrupted industries, and changed our lives with technologies. As ours became a civilization fueled by selling "stuff," design was the means by which that stuff was created. And just as the nature of business has changed radically since Henry Ford invented the assembly line, transformations of the purpose and function of design have been extreme. These metamorphoses can be tracked along multiple dimensions: in the role and influence of the designer, in what is designed, and in design's intention and impact.

THE CHANGING ROLE OF THE DESIGNER

In the evolution of design as a modern profession, small artisanal craftsmen were overtaken by manufacturers of mass-produced items whose parts and assembly were reimagined and mechanized for speed and efficiency. Along the way, the object was disconnected from its creator's hand; the unique signature was erased in the interest of scale. From clothing to furniture to transportation vehicles, design and "making" became impersonal; engineering dominated aesthetics; "shelf appeal" to thousands of customers took precedence over meeting the needs of a particular person or use. Early professional designers worked in obscurity as nameless practitioners in corporate back rooms and cubicles, closely following strategies devised by managerial minds

The Role of the Designer

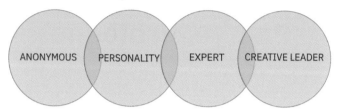

ANONYMOUS PERSONALITY EXPERT CREATIVE LEADER

Objects to Interactions

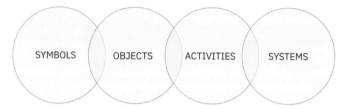

SYMBOLS OBJECTS ACTIVITIES SYSTEMS

Evolution of Responsibility

FUNCTION AESTHETICS ENVIRONMENTAL IMPACT SOCIAL IMPACT

WHAT   WHY

and delivering products with predetermined specifications, adapted to fabrication on the assembly line.

In the 1950s and 1960s, the groundbreaking work of a handful of uniquely talented people, such as R. Buckminster Fuller, Charles and Ray Eames, Deborah Sussman, and Paul Rand, changed the landscape of design. With their unique aesthetic styles, they proved the value that distinctive talent could contribute to commerce; with their highly publicized philosophies about objects, modern culture, and corporations, they transformed design from a craft into a discipline. Design became a cult of personalities with distinctive visions who raised the bar for how good mass-produced design could be and who brought it from the anonymous back room to become part of the C-Suite strategy. Excellent design was accepted as a competitive advantage, with the potential to catapult the company behind it to dominance.

A decade or so later, companies including Apple, Braun, and Sony and people such as Philippe Starck and Robert Graves created evidence at a global scale that design, in the hands of a visionary, is a strategy in its own right. Now, as evidenced by the success of Apple and similar companies, great design is synonymous with consumer loyalty, competitive dominance, and innovation itself. For the designers, both unknown and revered, who made this history, it has been a journey from obscurity to fawning fame, from implementor to inventor, from worker in service to business to the go-to resource for reimagining it.

Now, social designers are transitioning from isolated experts to leaders of change, facilitating the design of more healthy and equitable communities.

FROM OBJECTS TO INTERACTIONS

In the book he was writing when he died in 1983, Buckminster Fuller declared that the purpose of design science was

> to solve problems by introducing into the environment new artifacts, the availability of which will induce their spontaneous employment by humans and thus, coincidentally, cause humans to abandon their previous problem-producing behaviors and devices. For example, when humans have a vital need to cross the roaring rapids of a river, as a design scientist I would design them a bridge, causing them, I am sure, to abandon spontaneously and forever the risking of their lives by trying to swim to the other shore.[1]

Fuller is considered one of the greatest design minds of all time, but decades later, it's not just the formality of his language that dates his view of design's impact; it's also his romantic opinion of the power of artifacts to transform humanity in a positive way. Though he was prescient in his prediction that artifacts would become more important, his conviction about their ability to change problem-producing human behavior was innocent and afforded a view of only one corner of the picture. We have learned, since then, that what most artifacts produce is a desire for more artifacts: bridges, rockets, cars, airplanes, vacuum cleaners, computers, phones, assault rifles, and electric mixers. We have become conditioned to want them fancier, faster, more convenient, more powerful.

As the value ascribed to design grew, so did its purview. And as technology transformed contemporary life, design followed and was itself transformed in both function and purpose. Application of the design process expanded from traditional graphic and industrial design of consumer goods into specialized practice areas of hardware, software, user experience (UX) or user interface design, information design, virtual reality, and digital games. Each of these new applications required specialized expertise; it was no longer possible to be a generalist, applying a single vision across industries and types of assignments. But the desire for design, and the influence of the designer, only grew, with more opportunities for breakthrough products and services.

An area of expertise that emerged from the digital revolution is the design of interactions between people. Instead of creating designs that accommodate how people drive a car or hold a pen, designers began imagining ways to influence how people behave, how they relate and communicate with each other and how they think, what movies they choose, and who their friends are. For interaction designers, this opened up a new world that overlapped with anthropology, behavioral science, politics, and the design of culture itself.

The rush of changes brought on by technology meant clients were faced with the need to invent in areas and at a scale that was new to them and that required skills their organizations didn't yet have. Design, and designers, became the go-to resource. Designers were asked to lead projects of a scope beyond any prior experience, breaking out of the confines of the design department, integrating technology, human resources and corporate culture, research, anthropology, scenario planning, and business strategy. Suddenly, or so it seemed, designers were helping to imagine the future, reinventing ways to develop untapped markets or reimagine cities, cultures, industries. Design became the way to create the new.

Design is defined today as "the creation of something according to a plan." The ways in which design has evolved have been driven as much by its intention—what those plans are for—as by any technological or material breakthroughs or methods of manufacturing. In other words, it is the changing purpose of design that has changed the nature of design itself. This point can be argued, of course. It's true that new technologies and materials available to designers have opened new worlds of possibility for what is designed. They have also freed up designers more effectively in service to any purpose.

THE EVOLUTION OF RESPONSIBILITY

When Victor Papanek published his seminal book, *Design for the Real World*,[2] in 1984, he became one of the first practitioners to speak out against his own profession, laying blame on designers for overabundant, poorly planned, low-quality, disposable, polluting, resource-depleting products. As an example, Papanek blamed the 44,257 highway-related deaths that year on the poor design of the automobile. Although his criticisms of the establishment incited attacks from his peers and product manufacturers, even blocking his work from exhibitions and forcing his resignation from professional organizations, Papanek succeeded in launching a new breed of conscious designer and establishing his own legacy as the pioneer of sustainable design.[3]

Since then, a growing population of designers has been committed to making the practice more responsible, using fewer, recycled materials, and designing products and supply chains with environmental and human rights in mind.

Two other events continued the trajectory Papanek launched. First, in 2002, William McDonough and Michael Braungart introduced a biomimetic approach to product design with their concept of "Cradle to Cradle."[4] Until then, the environmental mantra had been to "reduce, reuse, and recycle," but McDonough and Braungart saw that concept as only a slightly less bad version of the larger extractive and wasteful economy (which they called "Cradle to Grave"). Cradle to Cradle is a model based on the way nature works, in which every by-product of creation is "food" for another part of the ecosystem from which it comes. Even for designers and clients who can't meet the demanding standards for certified Cradle to Cradle products, this concept brings a new level of awareness and possibility. It allows designers to use their talent and ingenuity to solve the problem of unsustainable consumption instead of making more of it.

The second event came in 2007, with *Design for the Other 90%*,[5] an exhibition at the Cooper Hewitt, National Design Museum in New York, inspired by Paul Polak. The title refers to the 90 percent of the world's people who live in poverty. The show was stunning—almost instantly changing perspective on the economic boundaries within which professional designers had been working and the potential that design has to improve people's lives. The show not only revealed the extent and extremities of poverty in the world but also drove home a point about the role designers can play in addressing it. Blinders came off; literal worlds beyond the professional milieu that had been invisible became impossible to ignore. *Design for the Other 90%* made the limitations of professional designers—dependent on clients who have the money to hire them and who give them carefully detailed briefs for what they should design—seem narrow and prescriptive.

This exhibition gained international attention and spawned a number of spin-off programs at the Cooper Hewitt. It became the subject of a series of high-profile articles and influenced curricula at leading design and engineering schools. The idea of design as a way to address human challenges took hold.

Inspired by new opportunities to put their talent to work for good, a growing number of designers began to rethink definitions of quality and of good design itself. Refined aesthetics, recognition for creativity or cleverness, and hefty fees as the hallmarks of excellence began to signal a former, unenlightened era. They were replaced by new standards of affordability (for poor people, not luxury shoppers), relevance to audiences who had never heard of design, and effectiveness in solving problems of inequality and ill health instead of only convenience. International health and development agencies became aware of the contribution design could make to their efforts—for example, what a brilliantly designed, affordable individual incubator for newborns could mean in reducing infant mortality. In small and quiet ways, among designers looking for meaning in their work and development agencies attempting to equalize the health and economic access of impoverished societies, a revolution had begun.

For designers, as the social design practice matures, it is bringing greater visibility, opportunity, and potential fulfillment. As it proves its effectiveness, the next step is to codify the social design methodology and make it accessible to everyone, so that it becomes a generative force in the world.

CHAPTER 4

Mastering
the System

AS IN THE PARABLE OF A GROUP OF BLIND MEN, each of whom touches one small part of an elephant and then extrapolates that detail to be the nature of the whole magnificent beast, social design is easier to grasp in parts than as a whole. As with any complex system, it's tempting to make assumptions based on the parts, but learning to see the entire system is a prerequisite for mastering it.

THREE COMPONENTS

Social design is composed of a set of principles, a process for organizing actions that propel progress from one stage to the next, and a specific set of skills required for the successful application of the principles and navigation of the process.

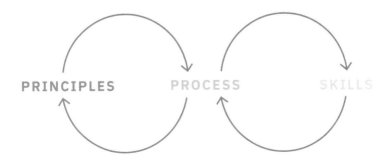

PRINCIPLES   PROCESS   SKILLS

Each component of the system of social design plays a distinct role, and there is a causal, symbiotic relationship between them.

Principles derive from values of equity and mutuality; they set the course toward positive (rather than destructive) change, guiding decisions along the way. Once internalized, the principles become a kind of operating system that acts as a common foundation for all participants.

The *process* is a sequential list of questions that, when answered thoughtfully, drive action forward toward a specified outcome, each uncovering insights that inform and inspire the next step.

Skills enable facilitators and participants to successfully complete the process, delivering on its intended objectives. They include the expertise required to take the process as deep and far as it needs to go. The requisite skills are sometimes possessed by a single person, but more often they are contributed by multiple members of the community.

Intrinsic to all that follows is that social design is social. It can't be done alone. Unlike other types of design or creating, it's not a puzzle that can be worked out inside one's own head. Therein lies its beauty, its relevance, its challenges, and its rewards.

THE ESSENTIAL PRINCIPLES OF SOCIAL DESIGN

This list of eleven principles is a distillation of the values and approaches that define social design and distinguish it from other design domains. Whereas the process is common to many innovative or creative efforts, and many of the skills required are essential to other disciplines as well, these principles contain the distinctive essence of the system.

1. Ideas come from the inside, not the top.
2. Questions are more important than answers.
3. Rely on experiments more than plans.
4. Creating is not the same as solving problems.
5. Limits inspire invention.
6. The real story is in the context.
7. How people see themselves is most important.
8. Innovation needs a network.
9. Communication is the first act of generosity and inclusion.
10. The process is the strategy.
11. Human capacity is the goal.

The Principles

The principles of social design are universal and inviolate. They are the beliefs that guide behavior, the reasoning that informs decisions, an internalized map for navigating uncertainty and determining direction through the unknown. Most of them create a tension with the traditional ways in which we're used to working.

1. Ideas Come from the Inside, Not the Top

Solutions come from within the communities looking to change. This doesn't mean that you can sit down with a group of high school students, if they are the community, for example, and expect them to know how to end violence in their school or neighborhood. It means that they know why the violence happens, where, and when, and what it would likely take to stop it. That will be far more reliable information than talking to experts who have worked somewhere else. The perspective and insights required to address any challenge involving communities of people can't be found in a conference room, a corner office in a high-rise, or the halls of an academic or government institution. They won't come from anywhere that excludes the people who are most directly affected by whatever it is that needs to change. This applies to managers designing new programs for employee engagement, entrepreneurs launching new enterprises, and global development experts working on solutions for extreme poverty in an ultra-rural part of the world.

This first principle is foundational to all others, and it requires vigilance. As obvious as it sounds, it's easy to forget, and it's often inconvenient to put into practice. It's comfortable and comforting to talk to people who already agree with us and who come from the same world we do. It's easy to think we know best when we come with an outsider's "objective" perspective that allows us to see issues more clearly than those who are caught up in them, or when we have spent a lifetime becoming expert in our field. We may have seen a hundred similar challenges before and think we already know the audience well. Perhaps we simply consider ourselves particularly observant or creative. In the short term, it can seem more efficient to decide what people need rather than take the time to talk with them about it, particularly if they're not fluent in the same language of culture, country, or industry. Social design requires remembering that it's simply not possible to understand what it's like to be another person, to have that person's challenges, or to know how to solve those challenges, unless we ask.

Any changes that are not transactional—those requiring the willing participation of the people expected to change—succeed only when designed *with* them, not *for* them. The best evidence of this logic can be found in the gap between the billions of dollars spent on employee engagement programs and the dismal state of employee engagement[1] and in the comparable amount spent on innovations for poor and unhealthy populations that have little effect on their poverty or health.[2]

This principle keeps us, and our work, alive and generative even after years of practice. Staying curious about cultural dynamics and realities that are new to us, learning other ways to see, feel, and know, avoids the calcification of "echo chambers," where people who look and sound a lot like we do reinforce habitual ways of thinking. It's an antidote to narrow expert status, an invitation to wisdom different from our own. And it's exciting because people who are not like us have ideas we've never imagined.

Examples of this principle in action can be found in the stories about Sisi ni Amani, chapter 12, and Brown's Super Stores, chapter 5.

2. Questions Are More Important than Answers

Einstein reportedly said if he had an hour to solve a problem and his life depended on it, he would spend the first fifty-five minutes thinking about the right question to ask, because if the question is right, the answer is easy. Whether or not it was actually Einstein who said this doesn't diminish its wisdom.

There's an art to framing the kinds of questions that lead to creative breakthroughs. The best are vague enough to leave spacious opportunity for ways to approach them, yet specific enough to provide traction for deep thinking. A common trap is framing a question that has a predetermined answer hidden in it. For example, in "How can we create a platform that will tell our story?" the highest-order need isn't known. Why create a platform? To do what, to what end? What's the point of the story? Questions with built-in answers limit options and shut down creative thinking instead of fostering it. If the highest-order need is to connect people with each other or to connect them to information that will benefit them in a specific way, knowing that opens the door to thinking about a hundred ways people might be inspired to seek information, one of which may or may not be building a platform and telling a particular story.

Powerful questions demand thinking beyond the obvious and habitual. They prevent the repetition of what everyone trying to answer them already knows. They are irresistible and intriguing when they're relevant, focusing a group's attention on the unknown. They unite people in the process of looking for answers instead of competing to be heard, arguing for their own solution as the only right one. Great questions uncover untapped possibilities and discourage prescription. They are the unassailable evidence of our agency—literally, of the ability and freedom each of us has to question the status quo.

A pioneering manufacturer of eco-friendly products had written a number of lofty mission and vision statements for itself and had a habit of using them all concurrently. The company had global imperatives that included "creating a just and equitable world," "inspiring conscious consumption," and "restoring our environment." Its mission was to "inspire a more conscious and sustainable world by being an authentic force for positive change." While everyone who worked there was proud of what the company stood for, the vision was so broad and unattainable that no one knew exactly how to move forward every day. If you're selling dish soap and toilet paper, how exactly do you act, day to day, in a way that makes the world more conscious and sustainable? What does that mean, really? Platitudes do not leave room for participation. Conflict at the company was common between people who thought their job was to help make money and others who felt that if they served the mission, business would take care of itself. When progress came to a standstill, a question was framed: "How can we become the first company to make being green the new normal?" Energy shifted immediately, and what at first had seemed both too ambitious and too simple to answer became a magnet for inspiration and collaboration. Pondering the question revealed truths that dictated strategy and the action required to realize it. The company would need to be very big and profitable in order to have that level of impact. It would need to make its products affordable to a majority of people in order to become mainstream instead of a more expensive alternative. Distribution would need to be broad enough to make the brand available everywhere, and products would need to be developed across a broad enough range to impact every category in the industry. Each of these future conditions implies the actions and standards for achieving it. They also integrate what had been two divisive agendas into an aligned vision.

It's uncomfortable to live with questions, and it's especially difficult to guide a diverse group of people to the quiet trust required to tolerate not having an answer long enough to find the right one. It causes anxiety. Often, individuals who are conditioned to like being in a controlled situation, or to take control, can't bear not knowing the next ten steps in advance. Western culture values fast solutions, quick fixes, instant expert opinions: the silver bullet.

The best negotiators are those who can longest endure the discomfort of not knowing which way a deal will go. They have the stomach to walk away from opportunities that aren't good enough, outlasting more delicate participants who "cave" in order to end the uncertainty. Living with questions works in the same way: those who can attain a comfort level with, and can even relish, the state of not knowing the answer, instead of rushing to find one, come up with more creative and unexpected ideas.

A good illustration of this principle is the work of Ruth Gates, in chapter 6.

3. Rely on Experiments More than Plans

Prototyping, which is essentially conducting experiments or pilot programs, is the only reliable strategy for navigating uncertainty. Carefully calculated plans are one of the ways we try to predict the future and give ourselves a sense of control. A relatively new idea in hierarchical Western cultures, and a difficult one, is that in the turbulent times in which we live, plans don't provide control; they don't work as well as they used to. The best solutions emerge from a carefully monitored iterative process rather than from strategies locked down in advance to the last detail. This iterative alternative approach is called prototyping. We take a step, pay close attention to what changed, and then determine the best next step to take. Prototyping requires waiting, watching, and listening, activities seen as far too passive for most driven executives.

The best place to look for proof of the power of prototyping is the living systems of nature. While nature's experiments are random rather than calculated, they illustrate the long-term benefit of taking each new step only when we know where the last one landed us. In complex systems or chaotic times such as our current unpredictable environment, the way that nature works can serve as an example. In the living world, random experiments take place all the time. Those that work continue. Does a longer tail make it easier to move through trees ahead of predators? Is a higher-pitched song heard more easily by a potential avian mate within the noise surrounding Central Park? If the answer is yes, that success is repeated.

For humans, making decisions based on emergent results is a far more reliable way to achieve an ultimate goal than trying to predict in advance what will happen. Prototyping is a way to adjust a strategy in real time, using evidence and observations of how well ideas work and how people respond to them. From the earliest stages of a concept, prototypes are essential guides to how to refine and evolve. Social design is never based on fancy predictions or guesswork. That's because when humans are involved, it simply can't be known in advance how well or even if something will work or be accepted until it's prototyped and evaluated. Through testing, observation, and refinement, prototypes are adjusted as needed so that by the time they're fully implemented, they've already been proven to work. Or, if they don't work, they can be abandoned without wasting a fortune in implementation. Prototyping is the alternative to rigid plans that, once implemented, are force-fitted to the intended people or place with disastrous results. The long-term benefit of that alternative far outweighs the discomfort of learning to wait, watch, and listen.

This way of approaching new models has found its way into business, where the Lean Startup methodology, with its concept of an MVP (minimal viable product) and the "build-measure-learn" feedback loop, is replacing traditional five-year business plans.

Prototyping as a method of acting in uncertainty can be seen in the case of the Salvage Supperclub, in chapter 7.

Three Stages of Prototyping

CONCEPT
A low-fidelity representation of an idea or hypothesis. This can take the form of a definition, a conversation, or any extremely rough representation of the concept. It answers the questions "Does this make sense?"; "Is it relevant and interesting to you?"; and "Does it have potential, and what would make it better?"
SOLUTION
A way to evaluate the function of a design and get reactions to the experience people have in engaging with it. Prototypes at this stage are medium-fidelity. They need to be detailed enough to simulate what the concept will be. The questions answered are "Does this idea work well?"; "What is it like to use it?"; and "How could its function be improved?"
WORKING MODEL
A high-fidelity prototype intended to answer questions that optimize the function of the concept. Prototypes at this stage help refine details, since they are as close to the final experience as possible. They help eliminate "bugs" and are done prior to full production or rollout. They answer questions like "Does this program or product or service work well when you use it?"

PROTOTYPING IN SOCIAL DESIGN

The purpose of a prototype is to make an idea tangible so that someone other than its creator can react to it. The benefits of even the simplest prototypes can be enormous. First, a prototype gets ideas out of our heads and off the pages of our notebooks and makes them concrete. That in itself is the biggest first step in testing an idea. If we can't give it form, in words or actions or materials, then it's not an idea that can be shared. We learn about our own ideas while making a prototype. We also learn from the people we hope will use the ideas. Prototypes start conversations; they give people a voice in the outcome. Finally, prototypes allow us to modify our ideas quickly. The expense of production or implementation can be delayed until we are certain that the idea works.

Because social design prioritizes human connection over objects, prototypes can take extremely simple forms. For example, the early verbal expression of an idea is in itself a prototype. Inventors know this well. They try out an explanation of whatever it is they're doing, present it to potential supporters to see what "lands," modify it until heads nod in agreement, and then adjust it to keep pace with the concept as it evolves. When Erik Hersman launched the first iteration of his rugged router, BRCK, he called it the Last Mile Connection to the Internet. The product and company have evolved to be far more than an Internet connection, but those words captured the essence of the concept at the time. They allowed people to react to where Hersman was going and contribute to or support it.

Prototypes help answer questions, and they are most useful if the question being asked is carefully considered and relevant to the current stage of development. Three common forms of prototype are described in the table on the previous page.

4. Creating Is Not the Same as Solving Problems

Both creative thinking and problem solving are needed in social design, but they lead to different outcomes. How to avoid the traffic jam that builds up every evening on your way home from work and how to unscramble a double-booked meeting on your calendar are discrete problems that can be solved, and solving them may require thinking creatively. But addressing the long-term issues of too many cars in a city, inadequate highways for the number of people who drive on them, and lives spent at the mercy of overbooked calendars requires a different level of thinking. The creation of new conditions that affect root causes must be addressed first, and then the symptoms that result from them.

Most of the time, problems are framed around the symptoms experienced: something is wrong or broken, and there is a desire to fix it or make it go away. But whenever human behavior is involved, there are invisible forces that cause the symptoms observed. Usually, focusing on making the problem go away brings only temporary relief. One symptom is eliminated only to have another appear in its place. Problem solving traps us in circles, chasing our tails, using the same level of thinking that produced the problem in the first place.

Creating brings something into existence that didn't exist before.[3] When done well, it changes dynamics at the system level, addressing root causes, while often eliminating multiple symptoms at the same time. What can at first seem to make a problem bigger ("Oh no, I just want to sort out tomorrow's calendar—I don't have time to stop and analyze how and where I spend my time") is actually a more efficient and lasting way to make the problem go away. Creating requires bigger and newer thinking and a vision with enough merit to become a North Star for all involved. It demands new questions and answers, fostering open-ended thinking about possibilities rather than acceptance of the way things are.

Jim Hodge spent twenty-five years at the Mayo Clinic as vice-chair of leadership gifts and strategic initiatives, and he is now associate vice chancellor of the Office of Advancement at the University of Colorado Anschutz Medical Campus. He is a perfect example of creating in action. He's personable, enthusiastic, generous, optimistic, and extremely successful at his job (which means he raises a great deal of money). He says of himself, "I have flown more than a million miles on Delta Airlines alone. I have made presidents, kings, and the Dalai Lama laugh." But no amount of travel or charm would make him as successful as he is if all he tried to do were to get new buildings built and chairs endowed. Although that would solve the problems of outdated facilities and limited access to the best faculty, as Hodge says, "That's boring to donors who want to think big and be a part of transformational change." So he listens to their dreams and helps imagine something at a scale no one has considered before. And in the end, they create new programs that, along the way to completion, build new buildings to accommodate their activities and attract the best faculty and partners to collaborate. Hodge says, "I help shape strategies around big, inspiring ideas that will be compelling to philanthropists." That is creating something new, not simply aiming to solve the problem of needing money, although he is brilliant at making that symptom go away.

The relationship between creating and problem solving is illustrated in the work of Interface Net-Works, in chapter 8.

5. Limits Inspire Invention

An expression used by sustainability experts, "tapping the power of limits," refers to the seemingly counterintuitive fact that the more narrowly a problem is defined, the more possibilities exist for addressing it. Concreteness is the stuff of creativity. For example, if a challenge is "Reduce hate speech and violence," you might sit around with a group of really smart experts and come up with some killer concepts that would, by necessity, be abstract. There is a good chance they'd be similar to ideas that had worked in other situations. But when the challenge is specific—"Stop gang X or tribe Y from shooting neighbors on the streets of Z in the middle of the night"— all that information, which at first might seem to narrow the options for intervention, opens up a far more actionable range of new ideas that are applicable to the situation. Because the ideas are place, time, and culture specific, they can be evaluated and then refined on the basis of feedback from prototyping in the context in which they'll be applied.

When undertaken without the grounding of specific, current reality, the creative process leads to too many possibilities and no way to measure their potential viability or value. All ideas become arbitrary. Deciding between them or evaluating ways to improve them is circuitous and enervating for a group to sustain. Using the limits of reality as inspiration and guardrails is the way to avoid this dilemma.

Erik Hersman and the company he founded, BRCK, in chapter 9, are useful examples of how limits can inspire invention.

6. The Real Story Is in the Context

Nothing alive can be fully understood outside the context in which it exists. A broken machine can be evaluated on its own to determine why it's not working. A water pump that doesn't function because people won't use it cannot. Nor can a violent or poor community be studied in isolation to determine why people who live there die needlessly or don't have enough money.

We now know that everything we make and do is connected to other things and other people. The clothes we buy affect the quality of life for factory workers on the other side of the world. The car we drive affects the air quality of everyone and everything alive. Buying a phone connects us to our friends and family but also to the destruction of mountain gorilla habitat.[4]

To understand the forces in play and the overarching system in any social environment, we study the context in which what we want to change occurs. What causes the existing conditions, where do the trails lead, where are the sources, and who are all the people and places touched? What invisible dynamics are hidden behind what we see, causing the situation or preventing it from changing? The process of social design includes seeing the invisible as well as the tangible, putting people, places, chains of events, and cultural dynamics in relationship to each other. Mapping these dynamics of context transforms unseen relationships into a foundation of understanding that can be seen, discussed, refined, and agreed upon by all involved.

Paul Polak's work in India, in chapter 10, illustrates the importance of understanding context.

7. How People See Themselves Is Most Important

Identity really is destiny. It is our assumed context in the world—our self-image as we perceive it in relation to whatever society, company, profession in which we include ourselves. It defines who we are and determines the tenor of our relationships. Individuals have identities, as do corporations, cities, and countries (and maybe planets, for all we know). Identities are the relationship between the outside and the inside of us: self-fulfilling prophecies, conformity to societal expectations, and the belief we hold of what we can expect from life. It's easy for people researching communities unlike their own to assume that the point is to know them well enough to see them clearly. That's true enough, but it's more important to understand how the communities see themselves.

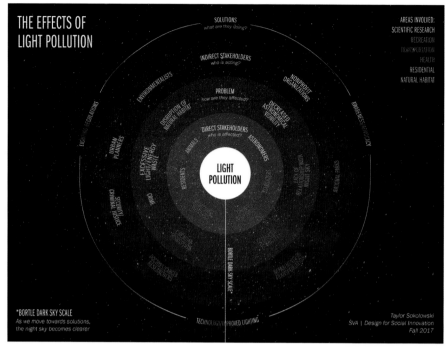

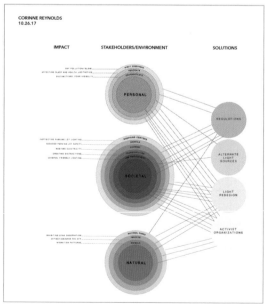

Map of the effects of
light pollution, from a class on
mapping and visualization taught
by Despina Papadopoulos.
(Taylor Sokolowski, Corinne Reynolds)

Nairobi has been called the Silicon Valley of Africa; young people there project confidence, a sense of expectation, of groundbreaking accomplishments to come. Artisans in Mexico have a different sense of their potential: as keepers of culture and history but not as creators of new value and technology for which the world is waiting. Entrepreneurs in Detroit talk about their anger toward and mistrust of the industries that abandoned their city; they view themselves as warriors fighting to keep their communities alive. These radically different identities form, and are formed by, different expectations of what can be achieved, and their stories' conclusions are contained within them.

Organizations and individuals who hold a vision of themselves as winners tend to win, and likewise with those who feel inferior. Places are like that, too. A spark starts, people believe it can spread, and so it does. Creating a new identity can have the same effect. The beginning of change is to feel, and then to see, that change is possible.

The current refugee crisis and the mass migrations that climate change is likely to trigger will disrupt not only the lives but also the *identities* of hundreds of millions of people—torn from place and uncertain (at best) of their context in the world. Where we come from is, to an enormous extent, who we are. Culture determines the food we eat, what we learn, whom we marry, and how we live. The place where we live determines our culture and so our identity.[5]

To succeed in helping communities survive in an age of disruption, we will need to conceive of and address identities in transition, with a fluid rather than fixed sense of what is possible. Obviously, this can happen only with the full participation of those communities. The way to effect lasting social change is by influencing a community's idea of itself: how creative it is; how collaborative, how empathetic it is; who its friends are; or how resilient or just lucky it is. The creative disruption will be to help engender balance—design as gyroscope, a way to keep things right side up.

The predictive power of identity is often overlooked as a leverage point for social change, but it can begin to shift the conditions of a community by modifying the way the community sees itself. What is the current collective or individual mind-set, and is it helping or interfering in achieving the vision? When it's ignored, a group's identity can foil the best-intentioned programs.

Jade Broomfield went to graduate school with a passion to understand and solve issues of racism among people of color. She thought she knew what the problem was, and she had a pretty firm idea about how she would solve it. Not surprisingly, as she

If black children are getting suspended more, leading them to fall behind in class, are always the ones into get in trouble with their teacher, and are looked to for problematic behavior, don't the conclusions their peers have come to make sense?

immersed herself in the communities where she was prototyping, her ideas about the problem, and the solution, changed. At first, she defined the problem as "colorism," which Broomfield defines as "prejudice or discrimination against individuals with a dark skin tone, typically among people of the same ethnic or racial group." Her research into previous studies showed that the roots of prejudice can be found in very young children and that it does lasting damage. Research from the Yale Child Study Center showed that black preschoolers are 3.6 times more likely to get suspended from school than white students and that teachers, both black and white, select the black students in their classrooms when told to actively look for problematic behavior. This learning shifted Broomfield's focus on where the solution to the problem might lie. She realized that instead of working on people's beliefs about others, improving the self-image of those who are targeted is the most effective place for an intervention. The graphic above illustrates Broomfield's logic.

Her theory was that since African American four-year-olds who have been suspended from school (more often by far male) suffer from a lack of self-confidence when they return, they need room within the school day to recognize their self-worth. This insight led to the creation of a program called Time In, a superhero-themed classroom program for black male elementary students who have been suspended. The program is based on mindfulness meditation and yoga—the latter turned into superhero moves

The Dumb Child

The Bad Child

The Unlikable Child

with the addition of a cape to make it cool. It provides space that "allows students to leave behind their suspended secret identity to practice their hero moves in privacy." Results were measured using a rubric of self-confidence, determination, leadership, and discipline. Broomfield was able to shift these four-year-old boys' image of themselves, to help them overcome prejudice and see themselves as worthy of respect and love. Her plan is to introduce the program in schools throughout Newark, New Jersey, in order to continue testing and tracking long-term change.

The principle of identity as destiny is evident in several stories in upcoming chapters. Jeffrey Brown's customers needed to see themselves as respected voices before they could become his valued advisors. Kenyan citizens needed to see themselves as capable agents of peace in their own right in order for the peace-building movement to work. And partners in Buffalo, New York, had to identify as part of a creative collective rather than turf-protecting individual entities.

8. Innovation Needs a Network

At any meaningful scale, creativity is collaborative—perhaps not the strike of lightning, but the realization or fulfillment of any audacious idea. Quantum mechanics teaches us that the relationship between objects is a greater determinant of their character than are the objects themselves. That's true of human beings as well—we are formed by the nature and quality of our relationships: to each other, to all nonhuman beings, and to the machines and technology that are an integral part of our lives. Our health and happiness depend on our social networks, on the quality and number of relationships we have with friends, neighbors, colleagues, and family. Likewise, our relationship to nature has been proven to affect our mental and physical state. And, not least, our relationships with the technology and devices we use affect our motor skills, our senses, and the substance and depth of our interactions.

In social design, the focus is on identifying and strengthening the relationships that lead to healthier societies and individuals. Understanding the needs and norms that inform behavior, and helping communities gain perspective on them, contributes to relationships of trust. Strengthening connections and opening communication supports breakthrough interactions in which people are more able to recognize values they have in common. This may sound obvious and simplistic until it is witnessed in practice—in the middle of Philadelphia's food deserts, in the slums of Nairobi, in large corporate cultures.

Even when this concept makes sense intellectually, it's difficult (at least for those of us in the United States) to act on, because it requires shifting from a transactional mind-set to a relational one. We are taught to measure, and therefore value, transactions. Investors, online retailers, and businesses that count clicks or sales as indicators of success all see the world in numbers. It's a clean accounting system, and with the right analytics, the organization always knows where it stands. Customers can be incentivized to do more of one thing than another, to choose one brand or movie over another, to buy the latest phone or service before they actually need it; but that serves only to solidify current behavior. In our personal lives, social media place value on transactions: likes, clicks, and numbers of friends are easier to track than the quality of friendships. Whatever the context, working at a transactional level cannot change the larger systems within which transactions occur.

Because we are interconnected, and because of the degree to which relationships form our thinking, it stands to reason that invention, at any significant scale, is not an isolated act. It is the product of a network of ideas emerging from multiple minds. All of our opinions and ideas are influenced by those of others.

The role of a successful designer has traditionally been that of a one-of-a-kind magician or hero with special talent who can be called upon, simply by plumbing the depths of his or her unique imagination, to deliver ideas more brilliant than normal mortals conceive. An architect or a product designer, for example, typically gets a commission, goes away to perform his or her magic, and then comes back to deliver the brilliant creative solution in the form of a building or product. He (still mostly he) is seen as a visionary for his point of view about what is timeless or modern, what consumers will want, or what will lend just the right cachet to a city looking to attract businesses or increase tourism. In this creative process, he doesn't consult or collaborate with the people intended to occupy the building, because his sensibilities alone are enough to determine what is best for them.

In social design, creativity is derived from collaboration among cohorts of people who ideally, in the aggregate, have a 360-degree view of the system in need of change. Within these cohorts, it is frequently discovered that what needs to happen is already common knowledge. In a project in Sierra Leone, for example, when ideas for how to improve maternal and infant health were sought from the health workers, families, and individuals in the villages most in need of it, everyone knew that in order for women to travel to health clinics, roads would be needed that didn't wash out during the rainy season; everyone also knew it would take more and better clinics to successfully care for a greater number of women. They knew that many husbands stood in the way of their wives' travel to a clinic because they wanted to keep them close to home. In complex social systems and institutions such as this, what needs to be done may be self-evident, but it will take a network of people creating together to come up with a viable, holistic solution.

Finding answers to common problems is also a collective act, not the work of one or two people in the group. It takes the combined perspectives of, say, villagers, policy makers, health-care professionals, and experts of many kinds to imagine different dynamics that might change the current state. Actionable ideas accrue through layers and iterations of conversations, notions passed along from one person or team to another. Ideas with the potential to help large numbers of people are both broader and more granular in scope than individuals can imagine or realize on their own.

A useful example of collaboration and networked creativity is the Buffalo Niagara Medical Campus, in chapter 11.

9. Communication Is the First Act of Generosity and Inclusion

The ability to make oneself understood, and heard, is more important than money or a big idea or new technology. Examples abound of ordinary ideas that, when presented

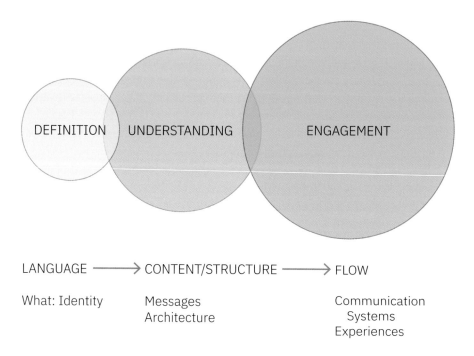

LANGUAGE ⟶ CONTENT/STRUCTURE ⟶ FLOW

What: Identity   Messages   Communication
                        Architecture   Systems
                                               Experiences

by a magnetic communicator, connect with large audiences and are accepted as sheer brilliance. We know less about the truly brilliant ideas that are presented in a boring way, of course, because no one notices them. Communication makes all the difference in what we know, what we believe, and how we relate to ideas and each other.

But the importance of communication can be found in its etymology. "Communicate" means to impart, inform, unite; literally, to make common. Communication is the essential way we invite people who do not think like we do to join a conversation. It's the way we begin our story, whether in a two-person conversation or a large public meeting, so that anyone listening can get on the bus and come along on the journey. Whether the language we use is verbal or visual, tacit or explicit, communication is the way we connect to each other. It's the circulatory system of every human ecosystem, team, or tribe, carrying critical information that allows people to think and act together, to stay together.

Alfred Edward Kahn, a beloved economics professor, said, "If you can't explain what you're doing in plain English, you're probably doing something wrong." Like all real wisdom, Kahn's grows more profound over time and when applied to new contexts. Many centuries earlier, Confucius was asked, near the end of his life, what his first act would have been had he ever attained power over the Chinese empire. He said, "I would rectify the language, and make words mean what they are supposed to mean again." These two bits of advice are almost all that's needed for real communication between people: choose words for clarity, and make sure we mean what we say.

The language we use to communicate has become, in the case of specialists, more arcane and exclusive, with acronyms meant to convey insider knowledge. Or, in the case of social media, more abbreviated, less genuine, filled with expressions meant to stand for other expressions. Special skill and practice are required in order to communicate meaningfully in media in which content is prescribed and hampered by limiting protocols.

Communication works in three essential ways: to define an idea or proposition in a manner that conveys it accurately; to create understanding by explaining how something works or what is needed; and to make a proposition desirable or attract people to participate. For example, if someone wants to form a new group or organization, communication is first needed to define the organization and its purpose. What's the point? What kind of group will this be, and for whom is it intended? Definitions are succinct and precise. Next, in order to make the group work, communication is used to explain the logistics, structure, and rules. When does it meet, how often, and where? Is it location based or virtual? Are there membership dues? Expectations? What value will people get from it? Finally, communication engages a larger audience by inviting people to join, or recruiting members. Words are chosen to sell or attract. Communication is easier to design when the role it plays at these three stages is considered and not confused. The sections that follow offer more detail about how each stage of communication works.

Whatever the context, communication, whether in language that's tired or energized, is the only means we have to effect change at any scale. Regardless of how big an enterprise becomes, everything begins as a conversation between people. If the conversation is interesting enough, it will spread.

Definition
All change begins with language, and if the language used sounds like what's been said before, nothing may change. It is the precision of word choice and sequencing that either

succeeds or fails to define an idea so that it registers with people who hear it. This is the most challenging phase of communication and the most important. It is also the one that is typically compromised by time or frustration with the difficulty of doing it well. Definitions are like acorns, which contain all the ingredients of a fully grown oak tree but manage to do it in miniature. Within large organizations, enormous amounts of money and time are devoted to initiatives that were not fully defined in advance and that inevitably fail or limp along for years as "black holes" consuming resources.

Understanding

Next, communication creates understanding. This can be thought of as the "kick the tires" phase. What kind of team will be required, and who will the team members be? How will the enterprise work, how much will it cost, how long will it take, and what will be its strategy? This is where the structure and function of a proposition are determined. It's an operator's manual that disseminates information to those who need it in order to make it manifest.

Engagement

Finally, communication incites engagement. This is the phase at which relationships are developed with a broader audience—all those for whom the proposition will provide value. Here, a clear picture of the benefits of the new idea, the role it will play in people's lives, what will be expected of them in return, and how they can participate in it are brought to life. This is where emotion enters—where the benefits of clear definition and understanding form the basis of communication that creates desire.

The Role Writing Plays in the Practice of Social Design

Nothing brings the need for clarity and specificity home faster than writing. One might think that the primary purpose of putting things into words is to enable others to understand them, but that is actually just a fortunate side effect. Writing is the best way for a writer to learn about himself or herself. It is a priceless but free method of self-discovery.

The hardest thing of all to write is truth: not the kind of truth in writing based on facts, or critical writing that refutes or supports someone else's theories. Not the kind of writing that tells an anecdote about something that happened at a conference or on the subway one morning. The most difficult ideas to convey are the unspoken truths that determine what we believe and, therefore, the way we behave.

Recognizing those truths well enough to put them into words is transformational for any thinking writer.

Writing is important at every stage in the social design process. Team members might think they all understand the vision of what they are creating, but until that vision is put into writing, it's likely that everyone will have a slightly different picture of it. Capturing it in words is the only way to know. It's also a great way to check in and get consensus throughout the process. Taking the time to confirm and capture progress in words realigns people, making it easier to focus action and make decisions.

Rachel Brown and her work with Sisi ni Amani, in chapter 12, illustrate the essential nature of communication and its central role in social design.

10. The Process Is the Strategy

If social design had a secret sauce that could be bottled, this would be it. Participation in a collaborative creative process is, in and of itself, the way to repair much of what is broken in inequitable and dysfunctional cultures. The overused expression that the destination is really the journey is not just a platitude in this case but a principle that can be witnessed in action in the space of a few hours. When diverse stakeholders engage in real dialog about their needs, and embark on a shared journey to create a new reality, it breaches the isolation of fixed, hierarchical roles. When the process is well facilitated, people learn new things about each other. Truth and aspirations are put out on the table and, in being spoken, lighten the atmosphere, in the same way an inrush of oxygen makes it easier to breathe. Common ground takes form, becoming a way forward in new relationship with each other. Observing a current state objectively and mapping it, without agenda, develops a shared sense of reality and enables us to see what's there, not what we want to see. Preconceived ideas fade away in the light of honest inquiry, becoming shared perspectives. What people have in common overtakes what makes them "other."

Participation in the creative process transforms people; it develops skills and capacity as nothing else can, with the incentive of taking part in the creation of something new. The process has individual benefits that last far beyond the rooms in which conversations are taking place.

In the process of articulating a shared vision, people gain confidence and learn to be better communicators, listening and processing feedback. Old relationships deepen, new ones are formed.

In prototyping, people do, and learn from doing. They get out of their heads and into their bodies, moving instead of sitting in chairs or at a computer all day. Moving awakens senses, which makes people more fully alive and aware.

Creating can take place only in the present, not in the past and not in a future time. Living in the present has proven benefits in relieving anxiety. It offers temporary amnesia about what haunts us or causes anxiety.

Making decisions on the basis of what is happening in the moment teaches us to navigate uncertainty and think on our feet; it gives us sea legs and better balance in uncertain times. Paying attention is the best instinct for survival, ever. We are more observant, fluid, agile. In his introduction to *Guns, Germs, and Steel*,[6] Jared Diamond makes the case that the average New Guinean is smarter than the average Londoner. The New Guinean travels through the jungle every day and needs to be alert, responsive, aware of random threats to his survival. An average Londoner sits passively on the same Tube train every day, lost in his newspaper on his automatic journey to the same office, largely protected from the dangers of the world. One lifestyle rewards alertness and awareness; the other makes its participants dull.

More than anything else, creating is satisfying, gratifying. It provokes an inner joy, a sense of self-reliance. It fills a void in ways that are benign and generative rather than acquisitive or destructive.

These are just some of the ways that the processes of creating and implementing social design are in themselves strategies for positive change. At a practical level, Michael Murphy and his firm, MASS Design Group, in chapter 13, provide excellent examples of how reinventing a process transforms its participants and changes its outcomes.

11. Human Capacity Is the Goal

The worlds of design, development, and enterprise are filled with product and service innovations that solve isolated problems for a while. Examples include a container to carry water more easily, storage bags that delay decomposition of harvested crops, technology that connects farmers to distributors and daily market prices, and text-based services that deliver vital information on prenatal care. The good ones have succeeded in easing the burden of carrying water, decreasing postharvest food loss, and improving maternal and infant health. In business, hopes and resources are invested in new products that will turn a company around, a single, winning hit that will open new markets, improve earnings, ignite a culture; or another line extension that will carry on the momentum of the original product forever. There is no such thing.

Isolated successes are isolated. They fix parts but don't lead to systemic or sustainable change. The purpose of social design is to improve human capacity: to infect and inculcate communities with the tools, skills, and agency to help themselves become more healthy, productive, and creative. That should be its measure.

As noted in the introduction to the social design system, these eleven principles are based on the values of equity and mutuality. They connect the process of social design to its higher purpose, and they keep momentum directed to the intended outcomes. With hard work and attention, they can be internalized, as in the operating system of a computer or our unconscious mind. They can then inform the way we process information and make decisions, freeing us to concentrate on what we're trying to do. As with a good tennis player, for whom form and responses are automatic, internalized principles of the game allow us to concentrate on the strategy for winning.

A useful way to summarize the social design principles in action is to look at how they differ from the current norms—how they shift behavior and thinking toward an approach that delivers more social value and more effective outcomes.

Finding inspiration inside the communities closest to the issues leads to more relevant, sustainable solutions than does force-fitting ideas determined by a group of "outsiders" who decide what's best. It's less convenient, and it requires the courage to deal with unanticipated answers, but it's far more interesting and productive. The failures of force-fitted solutions are legion in the world of social innovation.

The way to do this is to use inquiry as a guide, rather than trying to rush to answers without full understanding. Asking questions keeps minds open to better ideas instead of formulaic ones, and it supports collaboration rather than reinforcing the existing silos of expertise.

Prototyping is another type of inquiry, based on experiments that represent the concept at various stages. Prototypes provide an opportunity to get feedback from an audience in real time, and they provide a way of making decisions based on evidence rather than guesswork. Instead of relying on plans developed and estimated in advance, which most corporations or funders require before approving an initiative, prototypes are an opportunity to refine and change direction early if something isn't working, and to do so without the expense of full implementation. Prototypes improve our ability to make decisions when faced with uncertainty.

The Before and After of Social Design

OLD	NEW
Top-down	Inside out
Decision	Inquiry
Strategic plans	Prototypes and feedback loops
Solve problems	Create; then solve problems
Broad concepts, generalities	Tap the power of limits
Focus on parts	Map context
Focus on what we think of others	Focus on what people think of themselves
Expert	Networked innovation
Strategy predetermines actions	The process is the strategy
Communication is control	Communication is generosity and inclusion
Measure data and transactions	Measure human capacity

Most businesses, and even most traditional designers, work to solve problems—to make something problematic go away. Much of the time, that way of framing change focuses on symptoms rather than root causes. Creating is the act of bringing something into existence that didn't exist before. It begins with a vision of what that "something" is. When the vision is shared by the people affected by it, it creates the energy to realize it. Creating is a distinct process of envisioning and ideation, separate from solving problems but more important for bringing about systemic change. Many problems will be solved along the way to realizing the vision, but they will be solved within the context and in service to the vision.

Limits are an innovator's friend. The more specifically a problem is defined, the more creative will be the solutions inspired by it. For companies accustomed to making decisions from the top, this is a new way of working. It's related to the first principle of social design—of solutions coming from inside the communities affected, or "on the ground." When problems are defined on the basis of assumptions instead of concrete detail, they become generalizations, which lead to pat solutions, never real or relevant innovations.

The industrial model of business, which has spread into much of society, is that the best way to tackle big issues is to break them down into parts. In social design, the social architecture at play in any situation is vital to understanding real cause and effect. Mapping context is the way to distinguish between root causes and symptoms, to understand the best place and way to intervene, and to determine what the consequences on other parts of the system might be.

The way in which people see themselves determines how they behave, their capacity for change, and their expectations. It is often overlooked as the place to begin social change. Much of the focus of consumer research is on understanding and influencing people's behavior, typically their buying habits. However, when the goal is to increase human capacity for creativity and healthy behavior, social change has to begin with their relationship to themselves.

In a society, such as ours, that reveres expertise, it is assumed that nonexperts in any given area will be less able to contribute. Experts like to keep it that way. For innovation that moves large communities of people, collaborative, networked creativity ensures that the ideas most important to a community are the ones that will be implemented—and that the whole community will support the vision that derives from them.

Participation in the social design process changes people. Coming together, listening and being heard, and engaging in creating together evokes changes in attitude and gives people a sense of agency. That is both the method and the point. In contrast, the typical way that organizations approach change is to tell people what is expected of them, based on what a small group of experts has decided. The impact of that is to decrease individual agency and diminish potential.

In a hierarchy, communication is a means of control. It is the way to tell people what we want them to hear. It's a form of self-expression. It's also an indicator of status when it comes to who has access to critical information. In social design, communication is the way to share understanding and to distribute information so that everyone can make intelligent decisions. It is the way to include everyone in the process as equal participants.

Finally, though our reliance on data has only increased, all the data in the world can tell us only what has already happened. What should be measured is the increased capacity of people to be creative, solve challenges, and help themselves.

The Process

In plain language, the essential design process looks like this: (1) Be broadly curious and learn as much as possible about the context of what you want to change. (2) Make sense of what you have learned, and reframe the problem to be solved. (3) Come up with some ideas—more is better. (4) Test the best concepts to see what works. (5) Measure and evaluate the results, and then figure out what's next.

These simple, inviolate steps are required to create anything at any scale. They relate, to use a common metaphor, to the exquisite and immutable process of gardening: (1) Prepare the soil. (2) Plant. (3) Tend (water, weed, stake, fight off the bugs). (4) Harvest. No step can be skipped, nor can the steps be done out of order.

Social design differs by adding a step in front of the traditional design process. It begins with why you want to change something, not what you want to change. It makes the first order of business to identify the highest-level need. The next step is to map or measure current reality as fully as possible. To return to the garden metaphor, the first thing to determine is why a garden is desired in the first place. What should it accomplish? Is it to grow a few tomatoes and cucumbers for fun or to provide a reliable source of food for a big family? The answers to those questions inform all the steps that follow. The gap between that desired outcome and the current state (whatever reality exists at the moment) is a tension that incites creative energy. The purpose articulates desire, or, to put it another way, the purpose locates the itch, and the process becomes the way to scratch it. Actions are then framed within the context of the vision, ensuring that all the steps along the way add up to the desired end state.

An example is a project by a young woman named Meghan Lazier. Her vision was to provide greater mobility for elderly people and people with disabilities. The system currently available to this audience, called Access-a-Ride, was riddled with problems. Riders were expected to give the service a two-hour window for pickup, which meant they could never know whether they would sit in doctors' waiting rooms for hours or risk being late for appointments. On the other hand, once the van arrived for pickup, people had five minutes to make it out of their house—a challenge for anyone with mobility issues. Dispatches were unchangeable once they were given to the driver, so even if the service erred and was taking the rider to the wrong address, the route could not be changed once set. Had Lazier's goal been to fix Access-a-Ride, she would have accepted that model and tried to bring efficiencies and incremental improve-

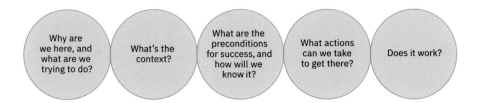

ments to the service. Because her vision was to increase her audience's mobility, her thinking wasn't limited by what was already available; she could imagine a wholly new model for systemic change rather than iterative modifications. Her ultimate concept borrowed aspects of various communication and transportation systems to imagine a service closer to Uber than to public transportation.

Applying the process is not as easy as articulating it. There are nuances and complexities, unexpected twists and turns, just as with gardening. There are limitless things to be learned if one aspires to be a master gardener, from soil composition to the history and preferences of various species and their adjacencies. Like the complexities inherent in designing with human beings, these simple formulas of prepare, plant, tend, and harvest distinguish sequential stages, but in themselves they don't provide all the guidance needed to propel action from one to the next.

What is transformational, though, is asking questions that must be answered in order to continue, as in one of those quizzes that won't let you advance until you complete a page. This exemplifies the principle that questions are more important than answers, or, in this case, more important than labels.

In the process described in the following sections, a series of questions direct action and drive progress from initiation to evaluation. When completed thoughtfully and thoroughly, each step is a source of power and forward momentum that leads to a set of insights, providing an exciting springboard for the next question. In reality, the process is circular rather than linear, repeating for each new phase of an ongoing initiative.

A core set of activities are undertaken at each phase of the process, adapted to the work required. These activities are (1) watch, listen, measure; (2) write, visualize, map; (3) think critically, develop insights; (4) communicate, engage, collaborate; (5) experiment, play; and (6) prototype, refine, measure.

WHY ARE WE HERE, AND WHAT ARE WE TRYING TO DO?

What are the conditions, needs, people, and influences that have brought us to this place? What is the need or opportunity that makes the effort worth it? Are we here to design a hospital or to create an environment that makes people healthier? Those questions lead to very different answers. What is the North Star? What is the shared vision that incorporates everyone's needs? How can we make it more compelling, more inclusive? How can we make it inspirational yet concrete and actionable? How can we say it specifically enough that we'll recognize it when we get there?

WATCH, LISTEN, MEASURE

Look for existing beliefs, resistance, relationships, arbitrary boundaries, and assumed roles of either leadership or powerlessness. Are all the voices that should be heard being heard? If not, how can they be added?

WRITE, VISUALIZE, MAP

Writing specifies both path and destination. At every stage, put observations, ideas, and insights into words. What's the story? Draw as well as write what's being learned. Build and refine the picture throughout the process.

THINK CRITICALLY, DEVELOP INSIGHTS

There is a critical difference between documenting what has been learned and developing a set of insights that propel the work forward. What does it mean? How is it connected or disconnected from other insights or prior assumptions?

COMMUNICATE, ENGAGE, COLLABORATE

Ensure that everyone has an opportunity to contribute and that information is available and relevant at all times. Establish protocols for communication or platforms where learning can be shared as the process evolves. Look for natural leaders in each community, and bring every group to the table to participate in discussions. Help form collaborative relationships by allowing everyone to see what is to be gained.

Don't rush to answer this first question or assume that the answer is obvious. Try on different "reasons why" to see what increases energy and provokes conversation. The answer to this question must be powerful enough to carry momentum and engagement through periods of difficulty and frustration. Having a clear reason why the process matters is often the best source of unity and purpose.

The designer's role throughout is to listen to pieces and assemble them into cogent language that captures the aggregate of what is heard and seen. Prototyping is taking place every time that happens and people respond, every time what's captured is refined. These early, low-fidelity prototypes are even more important than later, high-fidelity ones because they set direction and coalesce stakeholders. Presenting the vision to everyone who needs to get behind it can be done in a simple conversation or a carefully structured presentation. Create as rich as possible a picture of the desired end state, to ensure that everyone is seeing the same thing.

This phase is complete when the importance, urgency, and purpose of an undertaking are clearly articulated and agreed upon by all affected.

EXPERIMENT, PLAY

PROTOTYPE, REFINE, MEASURE

WHAT'S THE CONTEXT?

WHAT'S
THE CONTEXT?

Who are the stakeholders? The movers and shakers? Who has trust, credibility, convening power? Where? How? When? What are the invisible dynamics and underlying structure? What are the relationships between all the components? Where is value created, and where are the gaps and deficits? What can be seen, really, from mapping the context?

**WATCH,
LISTEN,
MEASURE**

This is the research and learning phase, also called immersion, and it's often deep and ongoing. Learning comes in many forms—from interviews, ethnographic research, reading about the past and the future. Most important is that listening takes place with an open mind, absent of agendas, and that all those who will be affected by the initiative are included.

**WRITE,
VISUALIZE,
MAP**

This is the place to map the current state or current reality. Capture what is learned from research and translate it into visible form that can be shared. Articulate the system so that it can be recognized by all those who need to engage with it. Show the hidden relationships, processes, and current and potential value. Map user journeys, value given and received, barriers, and opportunities.

What has been learned? What does it mean? What are the commonalities and differences in needs for various stakeholders? How do they align or conflict? Avoid falling back on labels or titles for the information presented; instead, capture what it means.

THINK CRITICALLY, DEVELOP INSIGHTS

Capture and translate all that is learned from listening to communities, distill it down to insights, and use these to contribute to a vision big enough for everyone to see themselves in, yet specific enough to define the action required to make it real. Find a rhythm for communicating that balances time for input from everyone with the solo act of crafting the words that express the whole.

COMMUNICATE, ENGAGE, COLLABORATE

This is an iterative process that takes multiple rounds of translation, mapping, and refinement to see what the words and images communicate. Try variations, from the expected to the audacious, to see how they connect people.

EXPERIMENT, PLAY

The map of the system is a prototype, an opportunity to get reactions and refine. Prototype the desired future state as well as the current reality. Find a way to quantify the differences between them. That gap is creative energy.

PROTOTYPE, REFINE, MEASURE

Depending on the size of the undertaking, this phase can last a matter or weeks or months. It is complete when the whole system at play and its dynamics are understood.

WHAT ARE THE PRECONDITIONS FOR SUCCESS, AND HOW WILL WE KNOW IT?

WHAT ARE THE PRECONDITIONS FOR SUCCESS, AND HOW WILL WE KNOW IT?

What needs to be true in order to reach the desired outcome in every dimension? What will have to be changed in order to succeed? What will success look and feel like? How will that state be recognized? What are the indicators and metrics?

WATCH, LISTEN, MEASURE

Facilitate dialog about conditions that will exist when the outcomes are realized. What are all the dimensions of those future conditions? For example, in developing the vision for the Buffalo Niagara Medical Campus (chapter 11), the team built a "picture" together of how Buffalo would look, feel, sound, and work once the vision was realized. What would it be like to live in the neighborhoods near to the campus? How would people get around, where would they buy their food, and what would they eat? What jobs would they have? What would journalists be writing about? It's not easy to step out of the reality we know and imagine every aspect of what we want to create, but this exercise brings dimension to the vision and helps confirm the actions needed to get there, as well as who needs to be involved in making it happen.

Represent the future conditions as fully and richly as possible.

Where are the priorities, and which conditions will, if realized, trigger others? What will cause a ripple effect, and what will be affected?

Seek advice and engagement from a wider circle of stakeholders and experts. Now that it is becoming clear what success looks like, help can be gathered from people who have done it before.

Try scenario-planning exercises. What if this or that happens?

Create representations of what has been envisioned. Use words, images, and interactions. Imagine how it will feel, and engage people who will be changed by it to get their input.

This phase is complete when every condition that must exist in order to achieve the vision has been identified and when clear indicators of how that condition will be measured have been defined.

**WRITE,
VISUALIZE, MAP**
THINK CRITICALLY,
DEVELOP INSIGHTS

**COMMUNICATE,
ENGAGE,
COLLABORATE**

EXPERIMENT, PLAY

**PROTOTYPE,
REFINE, MEASURE**

WHAT ACTIONS
CAN WE TAKE
TO GET THERE?

WHAT ACTIONS CAN WE TAKE TO GET THERE?

What are the things we can influence? What can we act on? What is the priority, based on where we want to go? What actions will have a ripple effect on the system, and what is the most efficient path? Who needs to be involved among those who know how to make it happen and those who need to be engaged in order for it to be sustained? This is the time to generate ideas—as many as possible and without restrictions of practicality. It's the place to let imaginations run wild without judgment. Once a surfeit of ideas have been generated, they can be evaluated on the basis of their relevance to the purpose, their relative cost, and their impact.

WATCH, LISTEN, MEASURE What information, opinions, and expertise are required to determine specific initiatives for implementation toward the goal? What happens when each action is undertaken? What changes or doesn't change? With the desired indicators in mind, how do the actions undertaken create movement toward them?

WRITE, VISUALIZE, MAP Define individual objectives, and document activities and plans so they can be understood by all. Create a visual representation of projects in relationship to each other; track schedules, budgets, and activities.

What is being learned through planning and acting? What does it mean, and what are the implications for moving forward?

This is the heart of project management, an activity in which designers excel. Become the center for information, progress, news, and coordination of roles and responsibilities.

Build time into the schedule to experiment, get feedback, and change plans. Avoid transitioning to automatic implementation mode. Embed creativity into action.

As often as needed, prototype with users, creating real-time feedback loops that improve the end results.

This phase is complete when there is a clear and exciting series of interconnected ideas for action that, in combination, will achieve the desired outcomes. These will be defined within the scope of what can be effected by the participants involved.

THINK CRITICALLY, DEVELOP INSIGHTS

COMMUNICATE, ENGAGE, COLLABORATE

EXPERIMENT, PLAY

PROTOTYPE, REFINE, MEASURE

→ DOES IT WORK?

DOES IT WORK?

Did it get to the people it was meant for? Did they use it? Did it work for them? Will they continue with it? What needs refinement, what should be eliminated, and what would have been better if done differently? What can be measured over time? How can the community be prepared to become more self-sufficient? What skills, tools, and support do the participants need?

WATCH, LISTEN, MEASURE In use, what are the responses and how is the uptake or acceptance? What do people say; what do they do? Have they changed their opinion or behavior? Are the people who will determine its success involved?

WRITE, VISUALIZE, MAP Complete the story. What is the whole picture so far? What can be captured for others to see and build upon?

THINK CRITICALLY, DEVELOP INSIGHTS What has been learned? What does it mean?

COMMUNICATE, ENGAGE, COLLABORATE How can the learning be shared with the community, and how can it be used to build capacity? How can it be shared within a larger community for extended use and learning?

EXPERIMENT, PLAY What is the best way to communicate a complex and unique story to others? Experiment with different mediums, forms, and stories.

PROTOTYPE, REFINE, MEASURE How are results defined? What is completion? What has changed?

This phase is complete when an evaluation has been made of the initiative's impact on all parts of the system (mapped as the context). The purpose is to inform the next actions to take.

A SHORTHAND LOGIC TO KEEP THE CREATIVE PROCESS ON TRACK

It's easy to become drunk with the thrill of generating ideas, with the promise that collaboration holds and the learning and precise refinement that prototyping makes possible. We can become idea-happy, coming up with cool stuff because it's fun to do. With multiple collaborators involved and a multitude of ideas on the table, it takes a bit more work and a good deal of discipline to keep the ship headed where you want to go.

Strategic Path

Following the simple logic outlined here creates the conditions for maximum creativity and collaboration and keeps the experimentation on track to achieve the ultimate vision.

Define a North Star. Keep it on the wall or on your forehead.

What is the highest-order reason for the initiative or enterprise? Why does it matter, ultimately? Grand, abstract statements don't work here. Saying that the purpose of a program is to "end poverty in the world," "fix prison systems," "end injustice," or anything else that is noble but too big and abstract to provide even a clue of where you will begin is too vague. It lacks the concreteness of place, audience, and approach. For example, the way a government agency would approach fixing prison systems is very different from the way an organization offering mental health care would. Specificity about the approach helps clarify strategy. On the other hand, visions that are too mundane will lack any real purpose at all. A vision to "launch a successful product," "plan a kick-ass marketing campaign," or "bring communities together" is too tactical and doesn't include the reason why the effort matters. It will not sustain engagement. A viable North Star is specific enough to act upon and measure and big enough to motivate and justify the effort invested.

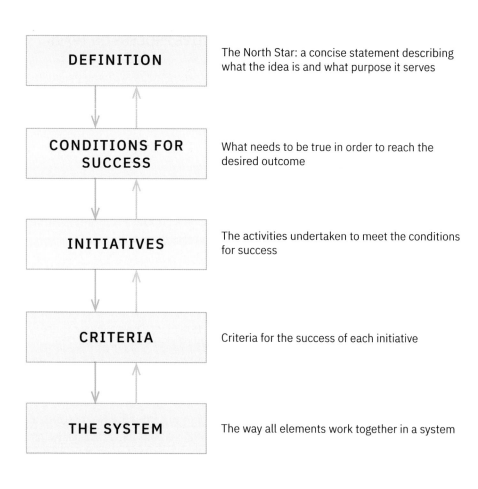

DEFINITION — The North Star: a concise statement describing what the idea is and what purpose it serves

CONDITIONS FOR SUCCESS — What needs to be true in order to reach the desired outcome

INITIATIVES — The activities undertaken to meet the conditions for success

CRITERIA — Criteria for the success of each initiative

THE SYSTEM — The way all elements work together in a system

Identify the conditions that need to exist in order to succeed.
What needs to be true? What will have changed? What will exist that doesn't currently? Who needs to be involved? This will take some thinking but will be worth it.

For example:

Our influence will have to be great enough to create a tipping point (in a specific geography or category).

Our products will have to deliver value at a price that enough of the intended audience (defined specifically) can afford.

Our distribution will have to be broad enough to reach our intended audience (again, specifically defined).

Decide what can be done to meet those conditions.
What can you do about it? What products, plans, and actions will create those conditions? This could include a product, a marketing plan, a different perception on the part of customers, or a different structure for the organization or technologies.

Determine the criteria by which the actions will be judged successful.
For every product, plan, and action, specify the characteristics or qualifications required. What are the performance and cost characteristics required? What are the indicators for success?

Map how all the elements fit together to make a system.
Draw a map of how they are related, how they influence each other. Include invisible dynamics such as value provided and information flow. What will the system look like when it's complete?

At this point, it should be more apparent where creativity can be applied to develop ideas that meet the criteria, and that accomplish the required objectives, to get to the North Star. This strategic path ensures that the time and energy invested will lead to the ultimate vision—and that every component will work as part of a system.

The Necessary Skills

Skills are needed in order to apply the principles of social design to the process. They are the facilities with which actions are taken. The greater our mastery of the social design skills, the more objective our thinking can be. The expression that "if you have a hammer, everything looks like a nail" has an inverse corollary. When you have an unlimited toolbox, your ability to evaluate and choose relevant action is unconstrained. Skills build confidence, resourcefulness, and flexibility. Since the problems uncovered in social design are often different from those anticipated, mastery of a broad range of skills is critical. Both hard skills and soft skills are needed.

Hard skills are defined as those specific to an industry or profession. An architect drafts; information designers are expert with mapping software; data scientists wrangle data by doing things with a spreadsheet that mortals can't follow. Filmmakers seamlessly shoot and edit what's in their imagination. As with any other profession, designers master a wide range of hard skills in their daily work, such as synthesizing and visualizing information or mastering dozens of software platforms. Typically, hard skills are the kinds that can be commissioned. Hiring an architect, a data scientist, or a filmmaker brings in expertise that others on the team can't replicate.

Soft skills are the "personal attributes that enable someone to interact effectively and harmoniously with other people,"[7] such as collaborating, communicating, and personal leadership skills. They are profession or job agnostic, and they determine to what extent people succeed in a work environment. Soft skills are more difficult to teach and learn, and they can almost never be outsourced to an expert or professional. According to Jeffrey Brown, soft skills are now recognized as being so important that they have been renamed "power skills."

The most effective practitioners of social design have a mix of both hard and soft skills. Because the process is so dependent on interactions between people, there is a social or soft aspect to every hard skill deployed. Experts of all kinds, when cocreating with a cohort, need to calibrate their own process to be inclusive of input from other members of the community. All high-functioning team members should be articulate about what they do and why so that the information will be accessible to the larger group. Soft skills are the necessary scaffolding that, when embedded within hard skills, allows expert collaborators to work together effectively.

Two things are important to note regarding the skills of social design. First, diversity of hard or expert skills is essential on a team. A mix of skills in business, social sciences, science, engineering, technology, policy, or any number of relevant disciplines is beneficial, depending on the project. The most effective teams are built with diverse hard skills but common values and soft skills, or power skills.

Social design requires six categories of skills that bridge hard and soft types.

Critical Thinking and Writing: The cornerstone, and the type of analysis that works against ignorance and prejudice, critical thinking is self-directed and self-monitored but aware of established standards of excellence in whatever is being analyzed. It requires thoughtful, cogent communication and writing skills, and it is the basis of unbiased opinions as well as agency. Any teacher will confirm that it's the hardest skill of all to teach.

Creativity, Problem Reframing, and Insight Development: This is the ability to reimagine, to adapt ideas from one context to another, to make connections that lead to unconsidered possibilities. It requires working with complex systems and reframing questions to uncover root causes. These skills are sometimes also referred to as novel and adaptive thinking or lateral, abductive, or entrepreneurial thinking.

Design Methods: The full design process has a series of component processes within it, including critique, facilitation, qualitative and quantitative research, synthesis, prototyping, game mechanics, making (giving ideas physical form or representation), user experience (UX) design, and communication design (and probably others). While some of these would qualify as hard skills, every aspect of the design process requires the ability to see, listen, internalize an audience's wishes or needs, and create something that incites desire—delighting people with the beauty or functionality of whatever has been created.

Collaboration and Collective Leadership: Recognizing and articulating common goals, leading others, setting strategic direction, and marshaling resources toward an intended outcome are also skills central to social design. These, too, are skills that can be developed only through practice. They require cultural literacy and sensitivity, communication skills, dialog, and facilitation.

Sensemaking: This is a bit of designer-speak, but it's difficult to explain with other words. Sensemaking is pattern recognition, but more. It's making sense of what the patterns (or lack of them) mean, determining their implications. All good designers have the ability to synthesize, to simplify seemingly chaotic and disparate bits into a form of logic. This skill is the basis of creating, mapping, data analysis and visualization, monitoring, and evaluation.

New Media Literacy: Not only are the language and form of social media unlike those of other types of communication, but also the way communities are engaged and attention is sustained is different. The design of social movements requires community building, network development, and mastery of all the skills required to capture the attention of an online audience. These are the gateway skills to inciting any kind of modern activism. They are a necessary component of social change.

In summary, the social design system is composed of a set of principles that establish the values and priorities necessary for positive change for all involved; a process for collectively determining desired outcomes, strategy, and action; and the skills required for successful implementation.

The stories in the chapters that follow illustrate this system in action. Each highlights one or two principles in order to examine them in detail, but every component of the system can be discovered in all of the cases.

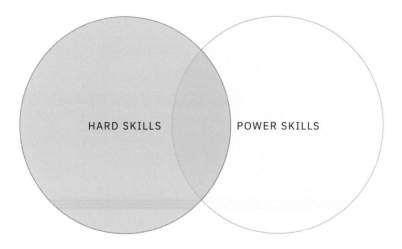

HARD SKILLS

POWER SKILLS

EXPERT SKILLS
Design, business, science,
economics, etc.

SKILLS OF THE FUTURE
Critical thinking, collaboration,
communication, cross-cultural
literacy

Nine Stories of Leadership by Design

CHAPTER 5

Brown's Super Stores

Solutions Inspired by the People Who Need Them

THREE DAYS A WEEK, JEFFREY BROWN WANDERS THE AISLES of grocery stores, through the dairy department and frozen food, the cereals and snacks, the produce. He watches what people choose to eat, whether and how they read ingredient labels, whether they find what they want. He lunches at simple tables near salad bars and prepared-food stalls, making himself available for whatever conversations people want to start. Brown is a one-man customer service center, but instead of doling out rote responses meant to end interactions as efficiently as possible, Brown makes sure his encounters are real dialogs, always in person, sometimes personal, and often begun or ended with a big hug. This is how Jeffrey Brown leads, by working with the people he serves.

He has built an empire from these relationships and the insights they've inspired. A fourth-generation grocer, Brown now runs one of the largest supermarket businesses in Philadelphia: $600 million in sales and counting, with some three thousand employees. He is chairman of the State of Pennsylvania Workforce Development Board, the Philadelphia Youth Network, and the Pennsylvania Food Merchants Association. He's been an advisor to both Barack and Michelle Obama.

Brown's Super Stores is part of the ShopRite cooperatively owned national organization. From a distance, it looks like other successful enterprises. The business has grown steadily and makes a profit. The team is adept at marketing and sales, operations, and customer service. The way it grows can seem conventional as well: expanding into new markets, testing and adding new products and services, doing more of what works and phasing out what doesn't. Upon closer inspection, though, contradictions emerge. Brown's Super Stores turns the accepted wisdom about American enterprise upside down: its locations are not prime; its customers are not affluent. The company breaks the rules about how a smart business behaves, taking on problems far beyond its core business and outside its comfort zone. That's when it becomes apparent that Jeffrey Brown isn't ultimately in the business of selling groceries at all. He is in the business of ending poverty and its side effects. Building a successful grocery empire is simply the way he does that.

It is this hidden higher purpose behind the explicit one (in Brown's case, growing a successful grocery empire) that distinguishes social designers. They combine traditional business success with an audacious intention to create greater social value, and they view what they do as the means rather than an end in itself. Like any elegant, systemic creative solution, this is a virtuous circle. Brown would not be effective in tackling poverty if he didn't have the granular insider's view of its causes and the opportunities that his stores provide; and his business would not be successful if it didn't go beyond exchanging money for products to help his customers thrive. Looking for the ultimate "why" behind any enterprise is a useful way to understand successful social design in action.

The neighborhoods Brown's Super Stores enters and succeeds in are those from which others run, in places where it's been repeatedly "proven" that no real business can survive. They are places where median income is $25,000 per year and far too many people have criminal records that prevent them from getting jobs; where crime and violence live up to their statistics; and where potato chips are for breakfast because there's nothing else to eat. Jeffrey Brown has made these challenges his business.

Simply by asking them, Jeffrey Brown has discovered that poor people want to buy the things they want to buy: the brands they recognize, the ingredients their favorite family recipes call for, with uncompromised selections of quality and sizes. They want to shop in stores that are clean and attractive, staffed by people who treat them with respect. He's also discovered that when customers are listened to and provided with what they want, a superstore can help address structural poverty and poor health as well as hunger, that it can offer second chances to former inmates who've been taught by experience they will never get a break.

With necessity as inspiration, Brown developed innovative financial structures to support a business empire selling things more expensive than its customers can afford, and started a school for formerly incarcerated employees. All of this is now available to other cities through a nonprofit consulting arm called Uplift.

What's most remarkable about Jeffrey Brown as a person is his courage, not because he works in dangerous neighborhoods but because he's not afraid to uncover problems bigger than those he knows how to solve. This is another common characteristic of great social designers. A willingness to eschew preconceived conclusions, and look for what is "there" instead of what is expected, requires fearlessness—confidence in the resourcefulness and resilience of one's team and the tenacity to find an answer to whatever problem is uncovered. Brown has learned that if you ask people what they want and what's bothering them, you can't be afraid of what you'll hear. His relish of new challenges shows up more than once in the same conversation, whether he's talking about obesity, the number of guns in a neighborhood, or the burdens of the formerly incarcerated. "That sounded like a problem that could be solved," he says.

It was at a gathering of grocers from across the state of Pennsylvania where the defining problem and opportunity first emerged. Someone pointed out that the average life span is up to twenty years less for people who live in neighborhoods without suburban-quality grocery stores, and someone else tried to unload a store in just such a neighborhood because there was "absolutely no way to make it work." When Brown expressed interest in buying it, he was advised to "walk away" from this guaranteed failure with its intractable people and complex issues. "You're young," the seller said, implying that Brown shouldn't launch his career with a failure. "This is someone else's problem." That was when Brown decided to make it his own.

But instead of assuming that he, as someone who had grown up in the business with a father and grandfather to show him the ropes, already had all the answers, Brown wanted to know why the last owner had failed. He invited everyone in the community to a meeting, as many as would come. He included not only the local ministers and NAACP representatives he already knew but also the "divisive" voices and the skeptics; all the people who could impact his success or failure were invited into the "tent." This first decision was, for Brown, as for anyone else intent on improving lives, the defining one: whether to retreat to the safety of one's own environment and confer with a like-minded expert team or venture into the unknown to ask questions and be willing to hear unanticipated, and often unwanted, answers. In social design, it's important to first identify and then question all assumptions—in this case, the "way things are done," or the common sense of the grocery business. It's a matter of questioning your own and your industry's beliefs and mental models instead of assuming that something or someone else is at fault. It requires tolerating things that make you uncomfortable, being willing to question the status quo even when it threatens the foundations of your enterprise. Most of the time, when leaders say they want to change things, they mean they want to change anything and everything except themselves and the structures upon which their power is built.

The first obstacle to emerge at the gathering in Southwest Philadelphia was the cynicism engendered by the prospect of "another great white hope" showing up with answers and preconceived opinions that residents had heard so many times before. When local community leaders stepped in and asked people to be patient long enough to listen, they began to sense a different character in Brown, to trust him enough to tell him why the last business owner, who thought he had all the answers, failed.

"The owner assumed we were criminals," they said, "and they treated us that way." Beauty products were displayed behind the counter, in a way that said, "We know you'll try to steal them if we put them within your reach." Carts were barred from the parking lot out of fear that if people could take them out there, the carts would "walk away." Security was obvious and heavy-handed. Employees sent to work in that location were perceived as "leftovers," after the best people had been sent to richer neighborhoods. In general, they thought, the store was stocked and staffed "like we're inferior people." They wanted first-quality products, choice, and service. That, Brown says, was evidence that the last owner had failed even the basics of quality, cleanliness, and service, the essential requirements of running a good grocery store.

But there was more. "We're from North Africa," some said. "We don't eat the food that was sold in that store." Or "We're Muslim, and there was no halal." In addition to basic insufficiencies, the previous store owner was ignorant of, and disinterested in, what his potential customers wanted to eat.

Brown left the meeting with not only an understanding of what was needed but also a good sense of the innovation it would take to deliver it. "There is a gap," he says. "When people want the same products affluent people buy but don't have the money to pay for them, that's a nonstarter for a business." In 2000, the Clinton administration initiated the New Markets Tax Credit Program, specifically intended to attract private investment to distressed communities. Brown was one of the first

Above: Anita Anim, MPH, RD, LDN, an Uplift dietitian, shows Major and Hannah Ashlock how to determine whether a product is made with whole grains by reading the nutrition facts label. *(Audrey Fish)*

Left: Jeffrey Brown poses in one of his stores with a customer who has shopped in three generations of his family's grocery chain. *(Brown's Super Stores)*

Top: At an in-store cooking class taught by nutrition educators from the Health Promotion Council, Alyssa Mills, a La Salle University dietetic intern, shows a participant how to properly peel and chop fresh garlic. In the class, called "A Taste of African Heritage Cooking," participants prepared the Oldways Caribbean Coconut Red Bean recipe. *(Anita Anim)*

Bottom: Learning the ins and outs of the grocery business at the Uplift training program.

businessmen to utilize this new program. From it, he designed a public-private part-nership to close the gap between the desires and means of his customers. And he began his first prototype.

The path from that first store to today has been a regular rhythm of inquiry and dialog with the people in the communities where he does business, followed by ex-periments in overcoming the problems and meeting the needs he's heard about. Typ-ically, some of the needs uncovered fall within the purview of a grocery superstore, while others are far beyond. It is the rhythm of prototypes and refinement based on feedback from customers that is essential to the social design process.

Neighbors are proud of the role they play in the success of Brown's Super Stores, and they want to continue to help guide Brown's progress. When Brown and his teams intend to try something risky, they start with a town hall meeting in the neighborhood where it's planned. He tells people what he's thinking and asks if he's on the right track. The power of giving people agency is infectious. Meetings have become so pop-ular that it's often difficult to find a venue large enough to hold the thousands of peo-ple who attend.

In one meeting, a woman asked if Brown had ever thought about all the previ-ously incarcerated people in the neighborhoods. "Your business is limited by the fact that a lot of people you serve are former inmates who can't get jobs," she said. "If they can't get jobs, they can't buy your products." Though he had never considered becoming the person to tackle it, this was one of the times he said, "That seems like a problem that can be solved." With nowhere to turn for advice, he hired half a dozen "really great" people, many of whom had experienced the system from the inside and found their way out. One outcome of this conversation is Uplift, the nonprofit Brown founded in 2009. Among other services, Uplift trains people with criminal records to work in the grocery business and guarantees them jobs.

In a dedicated, spacious facility that's part classroom, part model grocery store with checkout stations and a variety of stocked shelves, about thirty students at a time come for training all day every day for six weeks. In addition to the hard skills required for the jobs they'll be doing, they learn the power skills they'll need to thrive in a col-laborative environment that serves the public. Having a job is essential, but it's not the only requirement for success; classes include coaching on the basics of banking and personal finance, with one-on-one counseling along the way if it's needed. Since Uplift's founding in 2009, enrollment has steadily increased. People who have "touched the criminal justice system" now make up more than 15 percent of Brown's Super Stores' workforce, from entry-level positions to department managers. The waiting list for spots in the program gets longer all the time.

Just as Brown's is in it together with the communities, Uplift is in it together with trainees. Faculty and counselors learn what people need and how best to help them in the process of teaching. The team members have seen firsthand the dynamics of poverty; for example, if you can't get a job and support your family, it's not illogical that you might turn to selling drugs. They have also learned that with the right opportunities, the same skills required to be a successful drug dealer can be applied to the management of a profitable dairy department.

Brown enticed a successful young banker to come on board to run Uplift. His previous job had been to open new locations and financial opportunities for the bank. Brown suspected that those same skills could be put to use creating new markets to serve poor people in troubled communities, and he was right. Atif Bostic is now Uplift's executive director, putting his entrepreneurial and financial training together with a purpose he finds far more fulfilling than working in a bank. He is leading Uplift's expansion, consulting with businesses in fourteen states, and some of the other 25 million Americans who live in food deserts, to help them adapt and put into practice what the Philadelphia chain has learned.

Uplift also partners with Brown's team, prototyping other ideas to help the stores become a cornerstone for good health. The stores have introduced on-site dietitians, who give aisle tours to anyone wanting to learn about nutrition and how to decipher the small and arcane print on ingredient labels. There are cooking classes, one-on-one dietary consultations, and regularly scheduled check-ins to see how people are managing their weight and diabetes. Government-supported health clinics offer care in two of the stores. Mini branches of credit unions, with free services, are on-site for anyone who can't afford to do business with traditional banks.

Experiments have included everything from whether healthier versions of traditional food will be accepted, such as fire-grilled chicken instead of fried (resoundingly yes), and whether calorie consumption can be reduced by rearranging food on shelves, as in putting low-fat milk where the full-fat is normally displayed (mostly no), to whether a grocery store can play a positive role in reducing gun violence in tough neighborhoods. The latter pilot, which came from another discussion at a town meeting, involved buying guns from anyone willing to unload them for $50 grocery gift cards. Results included 10,000 guns turned over to the police department to be taken out of commission. Although the program succeeded in accumulating guns, it was stopped after a few years because it didn't produce enough hard evidence that collecting guns is the same as reducing violence. Funders lost interest.

What's important to note with these experiments is that prototypes can be designed as small risks, without great expense. In contrast with traditional new product launches, which take months or years of preplanning and expensive marketing campaigns, there is greater freedom in prototyping to fail and to learn from what doesn't work. It's easier to maintain objectivity when evaluating experiments because no one's career (or next quarter's earnings) depends on their success. In the case of Brown's Super Stores' gun collection, although the program ended when no hard evidence could be found that violence was reduced, this shared effort between store and community offered important learning for everyone involved.

Good grocers are masters at evaluating data, and they have access to an enormous amount of it. With stats on everything that comes in and out of their stores, they know almost immediately if a product is selling or a service is working, whether an item is popular at a particular place on a shelf or should be moved. They know how that item did a year ago and, using historical trends, how it's likely to do in the future. But with Brown's infallible instincts for social design, he never lets data take the place of the feedback loops he has set up through his relationships with the people who come into his store. Data are how Brown evaluates the results of the pilots he innovates. He believes that the people he serves know the blueprint for success, for his stores as well as for themselves. "Whether it's on food consumption, exercise, or substance abuse," he says, "most of us know what we should do, even though we don't do it." And regardless of how successful a business becomes, it's important never to fall back on what we think we know instead of continually seeking new learning within the communities served.

Although Jeffrey Brown is skeptical that a business such as his can be scaled up in a traditional way—wasn't that the problem in the first place, that chains thought they could open cookie-cutter operations everywhere?—his philosophy and the principles of his approach are spreading. One day in 2008, presidential candidate Barack Obama walked into a Brown's Super Store unannounced. Wheat prices had gone up, and he thought there was a chance that the topic might come up in his next debate with Hillary Clinton (Brown points out, as would Marie Antoinette, that wheat prices have caused governments to fail). Obama wanted to do his own research in a place where wheat products were sold and to develop a point of view on the issue. The future president took notice of the store, of its uniqueness, the place it occupied for the people of the neighborhood and the services it provided to them. Both men got long-term benefits from the impromptu visit. Brown helped Obama prepare for the debate and continued to advise and influence him and the first lady, including inspiring her legacy Let's Move! program to combat obesity. In this way, through still another person (who happened to be a future president) willing to step into the on-the-ground reality of people he wanted to serve, the principles and practices that have driven Jeffrey Brown have influenced millions of other people.

Still a relatively young man, Brown is by no means finished. He thinks a lot about poverty, which he considers our country's biggest problem. He thinks about the U.S. Department of Labor, all the money it spends, and how poorly designed it is. He thinks about how the insurance industry is structured and why it needs to be that way. Whatever he decides to do next, he will continue his process of cocreating with his customers, looking for the questions that will guide him in the communities he serves, working through relationships instead of falling back on the industry's traditional transactional approach, and prototyping big "risks" through experiments with the guidance of the people they affect. He will continue to work on poverty, tackling issues that others avoid and seeing, where they see futility, problems that look like they can be solved. If a grocery store can be a means to solve poverty, what can other businesses willing to lead through social design do? And how much more successful can they be if they create social value for the communities who support them?

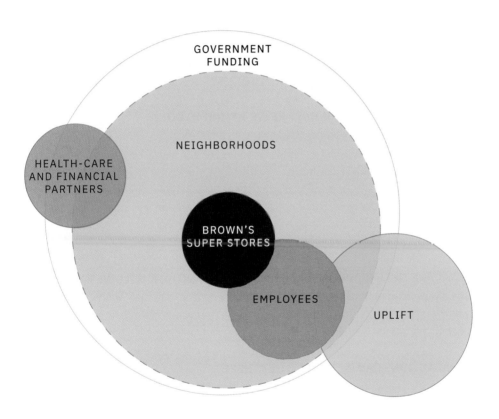

GOVERNMENT
FUNDING

NEIGHBORHOODS

HEALTH-CARE
AND FINANCIAL
PARTNERS

BROWN'S
SUPER STORES

EMPLOYEES

UPLIFT

HOW BROWN'S SUPER STORES ANSWERED THE SOCIAL DESIGN PROCESS QUESTIONS

WHY ARE WE HERE, AND WHAT ARE WE TRYING TO DO?
End poverty (rather than simply build a grocery empire).

WHAT'S THE CONTEXT?
The causes and results of poverty are a complex system that includes education, nutrition, obesity, diabetes, crime, the stigma of incarceration and joblessness, and access to benefits and financial services. A grocery store is at the center: it can impact lives and address poverty in multiple ways.

WHAT ARE THE PRECONDITIONS FOR SUCCESS, AND HOW WILL WE KNOW IT?
The stores need to thrive, customers have to be engaged, and their health and well-being need to improve. In the case of the formerly incarcerated, they need to become part of the economy. Each of these preconditions can be measured.

WHAT ACTIONS CAN WE TAKE TO GET THERE?
Provide the basics of cleanliness and service plus the food and quality people want. Experiment with additional services, including health care, nutrition, job training, gun control, and the like. Involve communities in every experiment.

DOES IT WORK?
There is evidence in the store's success, the people who find jobs, and the increased health of local residents.

CHAPTER 6

Ruth Gates
Mixing Science and Social Design to Address Climate Change

WITH MORE SPECIES PER SQUARE YARD than the most robust tropical rain forests, coral reefs take up less than 1 percent of ocean floor but support more than 25 percent of marine life. They are the nurseries of the ocean, and without them, the entire marine ecosystem would collapse. In addition to their importance to the environment, the global financial value of coral reefs is $9.9 trillion. They provide services through tourism and recreation, coastal protection, fisheries, and biodiversity valued at $29.8 billion. Coral reefs are essential to the economies and livelihoods of ninety-four countries. In particular, the Great Barrier Reef of Australia, when healthy, is responsible for an estimated 53,800 full-time jobs.

But the situation is dire. Fifty percent of the planet's coral reefs, vast edifices that have persisted for more than 200 million years, have been destroyed in the past three decades by modifications in the oceans due to climate change. All indications are of escalation. There is no coordinated effort in the works at a scale that can stop the abnormal fluctuations in ocean temperature and increasing acidity that are destroying the reefs.

Ruth Gates, director of the Hawai'i Institute of Marine Biology, has discovered what may be a solution. It requires her to prove a complicated scientific theory in a way that will gain the respect and acceptance of her exacting scientific peers, even as she goes against the deeply ingrained rules of scientific behavior. In both aspects of her endeavor, she is doing the unthinkable: breeding a "supercoral" that can withstand the effects of climate change while breaking the silos of scientific protocol to engage nonscientists in a global collaborative effort. Whereas most research scientists are satisfied with learning from their experiments, Gates has an agenda: an audacious vision to save the planet's coral reefs.

Like all contemporary environmental scientists, Gates is preoccupied with the planetary emergency brought on by climate change—in her case, for corals: animals so mysterious and complex that they may never be fully understood, and so vital to life in the ocean that we cannot survive without them.

Climate change is the most crowded and contentious issue of the moment. It is one that governments, conservationists, business leaders, nongovernmental organizations, activist groups, politicians, and millions of other scientists have taken up, each faction working independently from within the silo of its prescribed role. Gates's own male-dominated métier of academic research is constricted by narrow rules of engagement and the carefully prescribed scientific process. It's filled with competition among peers, storm front–sized egos, and invisible boundaries intended to keep science more pure than the messy human society beyond it. But Gates's purpose forces her to question all of these assumptions and toss the outdated ones. In an area in which so many people are at odds, she wants to bring them together, and she is using the power of relationships and a shared vision to accomplish that. She has become a networker and somewhat of an activist. In a high-stakes balancing act, she is juggling a scientist's responsibility to provide irrefutable evidence of what can be repeatedly proven with a social designer's need to help people imagine possibilities that do not quite yet exist.

Gates is asking questions here as well, not about why reefs are failing but about why some corals survive. She observed, after watching a series of severe bleaching events, or thermal anomalies, as she calls them, that not all corals died. Some were robust enough to tolerate hostile conditions better than others. Within large swaths of dead reefs, Gates discovered some hardy individuals that had survived. The question that drives her now is why this is so. "That is the story of my life," she says.

In the answers she's finding, Gates sees an opportunity to save coral reefs—to develop a superspecies through selective breeding that can withstand the threatening conditions that will undoubtedly escalate over the next ten years. But she also sees the larger context and knows that science is only one piece of the puzzle required to succeed. She knows that the world beyond her team and partners needs to join the effort. Her vision is to engage diverse people and align their efforts toward a higher goal, and that vision has driven her efforts as a social designer. Just as Jeffrey Brown uses a grocery empire as his way to address the systemic causes of poverty, Gates is using scientific research as the means to accomplish her goal of marshaling forces and voices well beyond the scientific world to help corals, the ocean's most important residents, survive climate change.

WORK IN THE WATER

Corals are intricate creatures: animals that have a symbiotic relationship with the tiny photosynthesizing algae, called dinoflagellates, that live within them and serve as an in-house factory for their food. A microscopic view reveals what seem like individual but synchronized personalities: during the day, the animal rests while the microalgae photosynthesize; at night, while the plants sleep, the animal comes to life—expanding its millions of armlike polyps with tentacles and stinging cells to catch anything that swims by. When ocean temperatures spike (called bleaching events), either the coral discards its algae or the algae choose to leave. Whatever the cause, without its food source, the coral dies. The result is a reef white in color instead of brown, except for the few hardy corals Gates discovered that are able to survive.

On Moku o Lo'e (Coconut Island), in O'ahu's Kāne'ohe Bay, Gates and her team at Gates Coral Lab search for the biological dynamics that cause this massive variation. By sequencing the genomes of the bay's five principal coral species, they hope to identify the genes that determine adaptability. As with humans, Gates says, coral's vitality depends on its own genes, the genes of its partner (the algae), and the environmental context in which it lives. Within all these variables, the quest is to cultivate, through selective breeding, a supercoral that can withstand warmer, more acidic conditions. The next task is to determine whether these supercorals can be used to restore damaged and fragmented reefs, increase the resilience of vulnerable reefs, and "green" the enormous seawalls formed by cement being poured into the oceans in an effort to protect shores from the escalating impact of tropical storms (the work that healthy reefs used to do).

Even in her rigorous scientific experimentation, Gates steps over traditional boundaries, thinking like a social designer as well as a scientist. She and her team use "tools drawn from the fields of molecular biology, developmental genetics, cell biology, biochemistry, organismal physiology and ecology."[1]

Twenty researchers in her lab create tens of thousands of corals, taking the very fittest individuals on the reef and deliberately creating unions. A severe bleaching event in the bay provided real-time evidence of hardiness and allowed them to tag thousands of corals that didn't respond negatively to stress. Now the lab's nurseries contain juvenile corals selectively bred from the most robust parentage. The researchers induce acclimatization based on the principle that "what doesn't kill you makes you stronger," in the hope of causing epigenetic change (changes in gene function that don't involve change in DNA sequence) in future generations. Gates thinks of it as bumping it up, giving the corals a bit of stress, making them run on a treadmill. The researchers use simulated future ocean conditions to evaluate tolerance. Against the accelerating clock of climate change, they race to work with generations of a species that releases its eggs and sperm to reproduce only once a year.

Gates reached her transformational moment after years of relatively isolated intellectual freedom in academia, which she extended through four postdoctoral research fellowships. It came in the form of a wake-up call to the hollowness of a claim she (and many of her colleagues) automatically tacked onto the closing of their research papers but never bothered to investigate. "I was writing this expression over and over again," she said: "This work has direct relevance to conservation and management of coral reefs." "How many times, really, Ruth," she asked herself, "have you written that statement? And do you really have any idea what research would be relevant?" In that moment, she knew it was time to leave the theoretical realm of academia and step out into the real world. "Scientists are really good at observing," she says, "but not good at acting." She recognized and questioned the assumptions that had been automatic and invisible: one of the first stages in the process of social design.

Since childhood, Gates has been drawn to the mysteries of the ocean. Her fascination with the televised world of star diver Jacques Cousteau triggered a desire to conduct her own exploration of the seas, and that grew into a relentless quest for deeper knowledge of them. For all that she has accomplished in a lifetime of scientific study, though, it is her compulsion to turn her knowledge into action that drives her to take on the challenge of convincing people from other milieus to join her cause.

WORK ON THE GROUND

Gates's next act illustrates a key principle of social design: collaboration and networked cocreation. In late September 2012, with the help of some academic friends and drawing on an idea she had, to use networks to activate science, she put together a workshop of unusual participants. In addition to scientists, she invited a group of managers and conservation professionals, challenging them to arrive at a common answer to the question she posed: "What should science be doing in the conservation of coral reefs?" It was a learning experience for everyone, beginning with how much about the other participants' ways of thinking they didn't know. Gates says she didn't understand the language of conservation, or of management, the decision trees and time lines that were so different from those she used. As it always does in social design, the process became the strategy: mapping and listening, uncovering divergent perspectives, was in itself the beginning of the solution.

In their time together, group members discovered they had conflicting needs regarding how to balance urgency with action, given that, in their respective fields, different certainties of outcome are required in advance. Where scientists learn to be comfortable not knowing how an experiment will go (the reason why, after all, it's called an experiment), people whose job is to manage the expectations of others within an organization, or among the public, need to be certain of what they can deliver before they promise it. Therefore, some in the group argued for immediate action to acquire the necessary evidence to take the next step, and others wanted hard evidence before they would act or would even be comfortable talking about it.

Different habits of language surfaced that distorted understanding and, in turn, complicated collaboration. For example, "assisted evolution" makes sense to scientists but leaves conservationists cold; "building resilience" makes sense to conservationists but is too vague for scientists and managers. Bureaucrats can get behind only the idea of "climate optimization." In communicating openly and comparing their different habits of language, the participants identified the values they share.

By the end of the workshop, the group had created a vision composed of eight projects critical to the conservation and management of coral reefs. Gates took on the most audacious one, and the riskiest, even though it was also the one based on a proven theory from Charles Darwin himself.

As Darwin argued when making the case for his theory of evolution through natural selection, whether it's for sweeter corn, blight-free tomatoes, faster horses,

Chris Wall, a Gates Coral Lab doctoral candidate, monitors a reciprocal transplant experiment by taking photographs. In this six-month experiment begun in August 2016, marine biologists moved fragments of two coral species (*Montipora capitata* and *Porites compressa*) between two sites in Kāne'ohe Bay to see how varying pH regimes would affect coral physiology, symbiosis, and reproduction. *(theoceanagency.org)*

Top: Pocillopora acuta polyps viewed using a confocal microscope. The red is *Symbiodinium*, the symbiotic algae that live in coral cells. The fluorescent green protein is found in coral (animal) tissue. The orange color highlights areas that have a blend of the algae and coral tissue between the polyps. The dark blue represents nematocysts (stinging cells) at the tips of coral polyps. *(Amy Eggers)*

Bottom: Close-up of *Pocillopora acuta* polyps viewed with a confocal microscope. Blue represents the stinging cells (nematocysts) at the tips of the polyps. Red indicates the symbiotic algae (*Symbiodinium*) that live in coral cells. The fluorescent green protein is found in coral tissue. *(Amy Eggers)*

Right: A *honu* (green sea turtle) on a patch reef in Kāne'ohe Bay, O'ahu, Hawai'i. *(Chris Wall)*

Top left: Gates Coral Lab doctoral candidate Beth Lenz pipettes *Montipora capitata* egg bundles into a culture tube for use in selective breeding trials. Red light must be used so that the corals are not disrupted during the spawning process. *(Larissa Franzen)*

Bottom left: Using scuba gear, Beth Lenz arranges coral fragments glued to plugs in a random order to prepare for a reciprocal transplant experiment in Kāne'ohe Bay. Marine biologists moved 3,200 coral fragments of two coral species (*Montipora capitata* and *Porites compressa*) between two sites with varying pH regimes to measure the effects on coral physiology, symbiosis, and reproduction. *(Shayle Matsuda)*

Below: A sea cucumber found at night in Kāne'ohe Bay. *(Raphael Ritson-Williams)*

fancier chickens, or better bird dogs, humans have been selectively breeding plants and domesticated animals since we traded hunting and gathering for agriculture, perhaps before. Where Gates's research differs from what has become common practice is in the application of selective breeding to "wild nature."

Gaining acceptance and active participation to put her discoveries to work requires the skills and principles of social design. Gates imagines, and is building, a collaboration among diverse stakeholders, a supernetwork with the capacity to act on what she is learning. She hopes the network can contribute not only to the scientific research needed to save coral reefs but also to the social and political capital needed to reach global scale. Her network is diverse. It includes scientists within and outside her own field and some unexpected allies: members of the hospitality industry, whose reliance on tourism will, she hopes, provide impetus for their participation; and politicians and government agents whose legislation either addresses or denies climate change. She includes indigenous people, whose wisdom and reverence for nature she trusts, to implement the ideas she and her partners are developing, and schoolchildren, who may learn to live with nature more respectfully than their parents do. Journalists and filmmakers who can bring visibility and, she hopes, support to the cause are also important pieces of the puzzle.

Her vision includes the formation of a supportive social architecture: a coordinated vertical network of diverse teams in every part of the world affected by coral reef collapse. A win will come, she believes, not from accruing resources for herself and her colleagues in Hawai'i but by inspiring teams in every affected country to apply their shared learning in the places where they live. She imagines engaged communities connected simultaneously to each other, the larger scientific and environmental communities, and the world.

Like every good social designer, Gates has become a master communicator. She recognizes the communication challenges her efforts face, not least because outside of scientific and conservation communities, people don't understand how essential coral reefs are to life on the planet. They can seem like something "nice to have," like a pretty home aquarium, tended only for the purpose of entertainment. Reefs are largely unobserved in the wild, save by island vacationers in snorkels, fins, or glass-bottom boats and a relatively small fellowship of shiny black–suited diving enthusiasts. One way she addresses this challenge is by both telling and showing the story of corals. Her website is a rich source of imagery, of "baby" corals on trays being moved from one tank to another or to a different spot in the ocean. From her room-sized microscope come stunning close-up views of what look like colorful arms waving for attention.

As Interface's Ray Anderson (chapter 8) did in his mission to stop the carpet manufacturing industry's assault on the environment, Gates addresses what she sees as an urgent need for transparency and awareness. She has an almost nonstop schedule of media and public appearances, "talking to everyone who will listen about the urgency and importance of this mission." It's a show-and-tell carefully calculated to convince audiences—from powerful policy makers and her peers to schoolchildren.

Gates says she knows, at this point in her research, that science will not be the limiting factor (meaning, of course, that her theory works). She also knows the kinds of controversies that could prevent us from saving coral: resistance from those who believe the problem will go away on its own (if we just ignore it) or who believe that some radical new technology just around the corner will solve all the world's climate problems concurrently. Some pushback will come from people who believe that nature will heal herself as she has in the past. Resistance will also come from those who believe that regardless of what is happening and the likely outcome, humans should not interfere in wild nature. This last argument is one that Gates finds particularly curious, since human activity has already interfered with every ecosystem on the planet in one way or another. And, as she says, "people who vehemently make this argument have no qualms about clear-cutting their yard."

Her work frightens people, raising concerns that it will create another freak invasive species, like the lionfish from Indo-Pacific waters that now live in the Atlantic Ocean and eat more than forty other species, or the emerald ash borer, an Asian beetle that has destroyed entire forests in the northern United States. Others worry that Gates is opening the door to a monster corporation like Monsanto, this time of the sea, that will brand and trademark genetically modified organisms for corals, making designer reefs and causing genetic narrowing. Still others worry that her work is merely fixing symptoms, distracting us from the daunting challenge of stopping the lethal behavior causing climate change in the first place.

Confident in the grounding of her scientific research, and with an understanding of the role that lack of transparency and coordinated efforts has played in past failures, Gates is not intimidated. She welcomes criticism because it means people are talking to her about her work, and talking about it, she knows, is the only path to coordinated action. In the past, she says, with her hands wide apart, "science has been over here and the implementers were over here. The Army Corps of Engineers was doing something unconnected to the science. That's when mistakes are made." She reasons that scientists bring a piece to the jigsaw puzzle, and every other part of the community has an important role to play as well. "It has to be a level playing field; they have to be concordant contributions," she says. "People have to listen to each other and collaborate, because the minute egos take over, the level playing field is gone."

If courage is measured by the enormity of the challenge undertaken, Ruth Gates is one of our most intrepid heroes. She has contributed immeasurably to our knowledge of coral biology, and her vision for the future of reefs is one of the few plausible scenarios we have. Beyond that are the important lessons her work holds for anyone with the ambition to take on large-scale challenges that require society and science to collaborate in aligned action in service to the planet and its inhabitants. It is cause for hope that Gates is showing us what's possible if we can overcome the false boundaries that prevent us from working together.

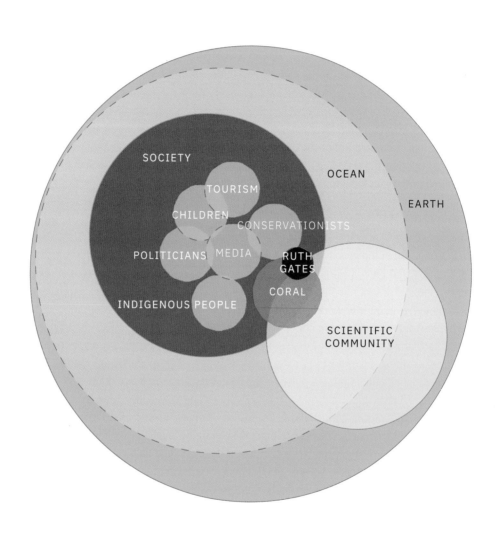

SOCIETY

TOURISM

CHILDREN

CONSERVATIONISTS

POLITICIANS   MEDIA

INDIGENOUS PEOPLE

OCEAN

EARTH

RUTH
GATES

CORAL

SCIENTIFIC
COMMUNITY

HOW RUTH GATES ANSWERED
THE SOCIAL DESIGN PROCESS QUESTIONS

WHY ARE WE HERE, AND WHAT ARE WE TRYING TO DO?
We're here to save coral reefs, using sound scientific research and social design as
a means to align the human resources required.

WHAT'S THE CONTEXT?
Expand the map of the natural ecosystem to include human society. Imagine what a
system that will successfully address the problem will look like.

WHAT ARE THE PRECONDITIONS FOR SUCCESS, AND HOW WILL WE KNOW IT?
The science needs to be proven, and it has to be adapted everywhere it's needed.
People have to know what's at stake, and the right people have to be "in the room"
to act. Each group needs to understand the value they bring and what they receive.

WHAT ACTIONS CAN WE TAKE TO GET THERE?
Prove the science. Identify the cohort of people with the will and wherewithal
to succeed, and engage them.

DOES IT WORK?
Is the scientific evidence conclusive? Does it work everywhere? Are people hearing,
changing, acting together? Are we still alive?

CHAPTER 7

The Salvage Supperclub
Navigating
with Feedback Loops

IT STARTED WITH A STORY, told by a buddy.

At an event hosted by a prestigious foundation, U2's lead singer, Bono, delivered a passionate keynote to a crowd of well-heeled New Yorkers, whipping up righteous indignation among them about the state of global hunger and how to end it. The buddy, working a catering gig that evening, was rocked by the collision of enlightened message and unconscious behavior: "The crowd was hanging on his every word. And we were in the back, throwing plate after half-eaten plate of perfectly good food right in the trash."

That story hit a nerve for a designer named Josh Treuhaft and launched his journey to find out what could be done about what he calls "the wasteful relationship we have with one of the most critical resources in our lives." It's taken him five years of almost fanatic dedication to see small changes, spreading like rumors, pockets of awareness that can eventually succeed in getting a lot of people—mostly in affluent Western countries—to question their assumption that if food isn't perfectly fresh and unblemished, it is not worthy of eating. According to the Natural Resources

Defense Council, "Getting food from the farm to our fork eats up 10 percent of the total U.S. energy budget, uses 50 percent of U.S. land, and swallows 80 percent of all freshwater consumed in the United States. Yet, 40 percent of food in the United States today goes uneaten."[1] Like Jeffrey Brown, Treuhaft is proving how even the biggest, most complex problems can be unraveled by really listening to feedback gleaned from small prototypes that keep designers' work connected to the needs of the communities they serve.

Food waste isn't a sexy topic. It's not something people like to talk about at all. Asking people to consider changing their eating habits is not particularly appealing, either, especially when the guy (Treuhaft) starting the conversation is snacking on bruised apples, dry celery stalks, and limp parsley. It can make anyone less disciplined feel self-conscious. Yet Treuhaft found a way to connect with people, inspiring them to rethink their shopping, cooking, and eating habits. Through a series of prototypes that evolved into a venture called the Salvage Supperclub, his frustration, sparked by a secondhand anecdote, became a newsworthy, exciting concept that has traction in America's foodie culture. Now in its fifth year, the Salvage Supperclub, a pop-up restaurant serving delicious, elegant food diverted from landfills, has expanded from New York City to Vermont, California, Oregon, and Japan. Dinners have been sponsored by global corporations, innovation hubs, and food-enlightened hosts and hostesses. The Salvage Supperclub's story has been told in *Forbes*, *Fortune*, the *Wall Street Journal*, and a documentary film from Discovery Networks, among hundreds of other forms of modern media. Another lesson of Treuhaft's story, like Ruth Gates's, is that open communication is the glue that creates relationships and the collaborations required for any idea to scale up.

In 2012, Treuhaft was working on the launch of a start-up in New York City that collected food scraps from restaurants and cafés in the city and delivered them to community gardens, farmers' markets, and other processors. These places would then compost the food scraps to create nutritious soil for growing. But the business was tough to get up and running. It was extra work for people to save their scraps, and it was hard to convince them it made a difference. Josh interpreted this resistance as useful information, a feedback loop that convinced him he needed to change his approach. He decided that graduate school could help him better understand how to design a business that would work before he took up his cause again.

Page 103: The first Salvage Supperclub dumpster dinner party: sixteen people dining al fresco on the Gowanus Canal in Brooklyn, New York, eating exclusively salvaged food. *(Tanya Bhandari)*

Opposite

Top: Composting is better than landfilling, but some of the food that's being composted is actually edible. We just need to change the way we think about what's actually edible and start seeing value in the things that we currently overlook. *(Josh Treuhaft)*

Bottom: A prime potato. If a potato hasn't turned green, it's still perfectly safe, healthful, and tasty, even if it has sprouted. *(Josh Treuhaft)*

This page

Top: Gazpacho looks vibrant and tastes fresh and wonderful even if the tomatoes had pockmarks. *(Andrew Hinderaker)*

Center: Salvaged squash rolls. A blemished squash is still perfect for roasting and rolling. *(Celia Lam)*

Bottom: Bruised apple and past-prime parsnip and potato soup, with a chive oil drizzle. *(Tanya Bhandari)*

FROM TREUHAFT'S DIARY

The Places His Prototypes and Feedback Loops Took Him

The following list is from a diary Josh Treuhaft kept as part of his thesis documentation for graduate school.

1. Posted "frozen food waste" photos on Instagram to see how much interest they would generate.

   Treuhaft's photographs of cherished garbage, reminiscent of Irving Penn's shots of unwrapped boxes of frozen food, won admiration as photographs but didn't move anyone to want to eat them.

2. Discovered the Ick Factor by conducting a series of eater interviews.

   Treuhaft learned that almost everyone he spoke with thought the conversation about food waste was inconvenient and unappetizing.

3. Pushed it further, posting images on Facebook and attempting to engage people in conversation about the limits of what they find acceptable to eat.

   Found out it can be pushed too far: that raising awareness about food waste can lead to feelings of guilt and apathy, especially in the absence of a motivating solution or alternative.

4. Pivot. Waste was going nowhere. Found an alternative: food.

   The big shift in his thinking came when he realized it was more engaging for people to talk about the food they like to cook and eat rather than try to wrap their heads around not wasting it.

5. The turnaround. Almost accidentally found a way to engage foodies.

   Liz (then fiancée, now wife) was juicing vegetables. Josh tried to eat the leftover pulp. Found it inedible (for him, this is saying something). On Instagram, he sent out a shot of the pulp and wrote: "I tasted this and don't recommend it. It's dry and bitter. Anybody have any ideas about what to do with it?" He got a bunch of e-mails almost immediately from foodies offering ideas. (Think muffins and things like that.) The lesson for social designers: questions are more important than answers.

6. Discovered the social side of food. Did a new round of research investigating people's relationships to food instead of waste.

   Insights: Cooking is seen as a creative act, especially when working with what you've got. Everyone has their own trusted experts or sources. Eating is a highly pleasurable, multisensory experience in a way that recycling and composting are not. Treuhaft recognized the energy people brought to this discussion and ran with it.

7. Prototype 1: A small makeshift dinner at school.

   Used the opportunity not only to test the concept but also to get people's reactions to names, cost, invitations. One invitation showed a man eating in a dumpster. That was the most popular. Bingo.

8. Prototype 2: Now named Salvage Supperclub and held in a friend's apartment. Expanded the audience beyond friends and classmates.

   Encountered serious enjoyment and support. Another lesson: when in doubt, try it, ask people what they think, and then refine your concept on the basis of what you learn.

9. Prototype 3: The final form: dumpster dinner party.

   The Brooklyn Salvage Supperclub becomes a media darling with a waiting list for reservations. Other restaurants follow.

Two years later, Josh landed on his big idea when he hosted a series of dinner parties with dishes made from food intercepted from landfills. The first one was makeshift, eaten at a dining table in the studio at school, cooked by a fellow student he had talked into volunteering. From that sketchy beginning, his concept went on to become one of the most exciting adventures in eating to hit the streets of New York, literally. The Salvage Supperclub, in its final prototyped form, was born at a long table set with china, in a swept-out dumpster hung with tea lights, on the streets of Brooklyn, New York.

The journey has as many lessons as the outcome does, filled as it was with prototypes, pivots, and eureka moments. It had the kind of fortuitous chance connections and unexpected partnerships that can be developed only when one pays attention in the moment and acts spontaneously as opportunities are uncovered along the way.

USING PROTOTYPES INSTEAD OF PLANS

According to Treuhaft, the single most important factors in his success were his "feedback loops"—the open two-way channels of social media posts, prototypes, and experiments he established with the people whose behavior he was trying to influence. His model is an illustration of how low-cost, quick pilots can provide far more reliable evidence of what people will buy—in real time—than any strategy that tries to predict people's behavior in advance. The opposite of an entrepreneur who comes up with an idea and then tries to create a market for it, Treuhaft had a purpose and used the community to provide clues for what design would achieve it.

Treuhaft cultivated a dialog that began the moment his quest did and that continues today. The conversation consisted of direct questions, requests for reactions and ideas, and subtle and not-so-subtle experiments in what was interesting or compelling or worthy of ingesting. He got "answers," sometimes in the dead-air silence of not being noticed, sometimes in an enthusiastic onrush of ideas from opinionated foodies, sometimes in the form of in-kind support for hosting or cooking or a place on the street to park a dumpster. Other feedback came from people's wallets. Time and time again, he assessed how much people were willing to pay for his concoctions made of waste. He paid attention, acting on what he saw and heard. Each set of responses shifted his direction and helped him refine his understanding of what inspires people to engage with food waste. As he monitored feedback and honed his interpretive skills, the reactions to his prototypes became a kind of GPS powered by human energy, leading him forward as reliably as Waze takes drivers through an unfamiliar neighborhood. Seeing the solution in its final form makes it easy to forget that Treuhaft had no idea what would work when he began this journey.

It's a difficult proposition to change the attitudes of privileged people, compelling them to view food left on a dinner plate as a sign of selfish recklessness rather than self-righteous caloric discipline. They are conditioned to believe that the "land of plenty" will be theirs to enjoy forever. Yet Treuhaft had even more ambitious plans: he wanted to convince people to open their minds and mouths to the overripe banana, the bruised pear, the misshapen carrot, the soggy mushroom, and the too-mushy-to-have-been-harvested-that-month potato, when they had been carefully conditioned by marketers to believe they deserve, and should have, only the flawless and beautiful.

Making plans one step at a time in response to feedback from users is a highly uncomfortable way of working for anyone who's been taught traditional business thinking, with its reliance on long-term strategies. It requires trust in the process—that the next step will be evident when it's needed—and trust in one's own resourcefulness and ability to make the right decisions in real time. When mastered, this way of working is actually more comforting because it is based on evidence instead of assumptions. But it requires that practitioners be able to live with that part of the creative process in which one does not yet have the answer.

Another lesson is an essential insight into human nature, evidence of which is omnipresent in Western culture in the form of consumerism and extreme ambition. We inevitably gravitate toward the new shiny object or delight or privilege du jour, wanting it, wanting to feel we deserve it (possibly more than others), viewing it as evidence of our freedom of choice. What we almost never want is to have something taken away or to be told there is something we should not do.

For Treuhaft, this lesson took the form of a dramatic revelation. After many months spent trying out ways to get people to stop tossing anything past its prime into the garbage, and discarding edible parts of food during preparation and cooking, he turned his theory around. He began offering people something new and shiny instead of trying to take something away. Specifically, he devised an opportunity for creativity, achievement, satisfaction, entertainment, fresh experiences, and membership in an enlightened community. In other words, he found a way to reward people for trying something new rather than requesting an inconvenience or sacrifice.

Social design is a dynamic cocreative process in which people participate rather than being passive recipients; in the case of the Salvage Supperclub, that includes

THE DESIGNATED DRIVER

One of the most dramatic examples of this human "It's okay to give me something, but don't take anything away" dynamic is the campaign against drunk driving. For years, public service campaigns focused on frightening drivers with stories and pictures of dead teenagers and those who lost them, on flattering sober drivers for their abstention, or on appealing to drivers' rational minds with statistics. Yet nothing worked. Alcohol-related traffic deaths remained the number one killer of fifteen- to twenty-four-year-old young adults in the United States, year after year.

Then, in 1988, a group of Hollywood creative people partnered with the Harvard School of Public Health to build a campaign around an idea imported from Scandinavia (the collaboration itself an example of social design in action).

They created the "designated driver," the person in a group of rowdy drinkers who takes responsibility for holding the keys and staying sober. The campaign's brilliance lies in creating special stature and a title for this person—giving the designated driver an elevated position instead of just denying him or her drinks for the night. Quite simply, it works because it gives designated drivers a clear role and the most important job within their group—saving lives.

By 1994, annual alcohol-related traffic deaths had declined by 30 percent.[2] The designated driver has been embedded in our consciousness ever since. Now he or she can be found everywhere, from cartoons of cowboys on horses, who need a designated driver to steer their mount, to a simple image of a set of keys being passed from one hand to another, communicating so clearly with that gesture that no words are required. This is the kind of powerful insight that comes from designing with human relationships.

chefs and servers; farmers, grocers, and restaurateurs who contribute "wasted" food; and, especially, diners. The benefit is that all parties have an interest in the success of the endeavor because they are a part of it. Just as Jeffrey Brown's customers feel a sense of ownership of the stores because they help identify opportunities, Josh Treuhaft's team and guests are invested in the Salvage Supperclub concept. They know that their contribution to the vision is to talk about their experience, help raise awareness, and get more people to think about food in a different way.

With the Salvage Supperclub, there is always a great story to tell. Hosting a dinner is as unusual an affair as attending one. The menu isn't planned in advance. There is no shopping list. It comes together as an assemblage, made from the food equivalent of precious objets trouvés. Treuhaft and his catering crew scout for fruits and vegetables that are on their way to landfills, earmarked for trash bins but not yet deposited there. They scavenge for overripe apples and peaches and broccoli stems from bruise boxes in farmers' markets, grocery stores, food co-ops, restaurants, hotels, farms, and catering companies. Only as the ingredients are gathered can the menu be fixed. The story of the quest then becomes an ingredient in the drama of the dinner party: every dish a tale of provenance, of the pedigree and preciousness of carrot tops turned into pesto or slaw made from broccoli stalks or "aged" zucchini butter spread on toast made from yesterday's bread. Each is presented with as much flair and pride as a waiter at a three-star restaurant would display while divulging the romantic coast from which that day's oysters were flown. A Salvage Supperclub dinner is so entertaining, unusual, tasty, and intriguing that people rarely notice that the meal they're eating is vegan.

Had Treuhaft's goal been simply to open a restaurant, the process would have been a very different one. Decisions and calculations would have been required regarding location, real estate, interior design, marketing, expenses, profits, and how many times a night it could "turn over" tables. Because his goal was to change the way people think about and consume food, he designed for the relationships that would lead to that: between people and what they consider edible, between his restaurant and its suppliers and patrons, between diners' friends and the people who heard the stories recounted.

In any endeavor with a social mission, it's easy to let the purpose dominate, to convince oneself that if an experience has a social mission, it can't be enjoyable or its seriousness of purpose will be questioned. Tedious repetition of good intentions and earnestness are the tools that most organizations lean heavily upon to convey their effectiveness and gravitas. The Salvage Supperclub is an example of the power that design has to delight, to attract and entertain rather than bludgeon. By locating his restaurant in a swept-out dumpster, with incongruously delicate hanging tea lights and a beautifully set table, Treuhaft made his Salvage Supperclub dinners instantly famous. He brought people together for a romantic, sensory experience: an adventure that transformed their trepidation about eating ugly food into a beautiful relationship to it, creating a memory they would talk about and never forget.

Observing the Salvage Supperclub from the outside, with no understanding of the way it developed through feedback and prototypes, one might consider it a dangerous risk to open a restaurant in a dumpster, serving discarded food. But seen through the perspective of how each decision was made, informed by learning from careful experiments, the startling end result is seen as a natural evolution of the process that led to it. In this way, social design leads to disruptive new ideas.

The most important takeaway from the Salvage Supperclub story is how small tests, refinements, and evolution of the idea became a real-time strategy. This part of the social design process is adaptable anywhere, to any issue and any kind of enterprise. If there is no obvious audience to engage in cocreating an idea, then something about the scope of the thinking is wrong. Concrete dialog is needed between creator and user in order to create a relevant design.

More broadly, Treuhaft's approach holds lessons for anyone attempting to shift a culture to be more responsible or engaged. Social design itself is composed of relationships with everyone in that culture. Like any good relationship, it is a two-way dialog, a conversational rhythm of putting ideas out, paying attention to what people say and do, and then going on from there to build a deeper conversation.

HOW JOSH TREUHAFT ANSWERED
THE SOCIAL DESIGN PROCESS QUESTIONS

WHY ARE WE HERE, AND WHAT ARE WE TRYING TO DO?
Change the way people think about food and inspire them to stop wasting it.

WHAT'S THE CONTEXT?
Culture itself. The food industry, from farmers to grocers to manufacturers. An assumption that we should eat only the perfect, and "common sense" about what parts of vegetables should be thrown away.

WHAT ARE THE PRECONDITIONS FOR SUCCESS, AND HOW WILL WE KNOW IT?
The idea has to attract people, not pressure them. A place to experience this new kind of eating has to be available. It needs to make news.

WHAT ACTIONS CAN WE TAKE TO GET THERE?
Create that experience and align all the partners needed to make it happen. Tell the world.

DOES IT WORK?
After they have the experience, does it change the way people eat at home? Do people who hear about it but don't experience the dinner think and behave differently?

CHAPTER 8

Interface Net-Works

Creating New Models and Solving Problems along the Way

SUCCESS, IN THE CORPORATE WORLD AND ON WALL STREET, hides many sins. It's an unspoken, and even accepted, norm that the price for growth and profitability in manufacturing is environmental destruction. The manufacture of cars, smartphones, and clothes, for example, has dirty secrets that are known but rarely mentioned. That's just the way it goes. If you want to make an omelet, it is said, you have to break some eggs.

Corporate language helps hide these realities in the kind of vague, committee-rendered sentiments that look nice but lack any real commitment. A trope that makes no specific promise can sound meaningful yet can either camouflage a corporation's blindness to its own real impact or, worse, intentionally omit its crimes.

To uncouple this dichotomy of success and destruction is a daunting task: one that requires the courage to question the way everything has been done and commit to the upheaval of institution-wide innovation required to change it. The carpet manufacturer Interface has rewritten the old story. The company is one of the most remarkable examples of transformation in the industrial world.

Interface demonstrates how a company in an industry that contributes mindlessly to the destruction of the environment can lead the way to restoring it. Propelled by the fervor of founder and CEO Ray Anderson, the company, then twenty-one years old, shifted gears in 1994. It transitioned from a typical, toxic carpet company to an innovative manufacturer with aims to leave no earthly footprint—zero impact on the environment. In the process, it wanted to prove that transformational corporate responsibility and enormous commercial success are mutually compatible.

Business as usual for the carpet industry shows a bleak picture of environmental destruction. A 2016 report from the Global Alliance for Incinerator Alternatives (GAIA) and Changing Markets, titled "Swept Under the Carpet: Exposing the Greenwash of the U.S. Carpet Industry,"[1] tells us that 89 percent of discarded carpet is dumped in landfills, while another 6 percent is incinerated. Less than 5 percent is reused or recycled, making carpets responsible for about 3.5 percent of U.S. landfill waste, or 4 billion pounds per year. And that's just volume. Synthetic carpets are made from petrochemicals, which means they don't biodegrade in anyone's lifetime. They leach toxic chemicals into the ground and the water supplies of the typically low-income neighborhoods where they are located. And, as a 2017 article reported, they "release persistent organic pollutants, endocrine disruptors, and other hazardous chemicals like dioxin, mercury, and lead," which lead to higher cancer rates, heart attacks, strokes, pulmonary disease, and asthma at the local level.[2] All that before adding up the industry's contribution to climate change.

Interface's simply stated but audacious goal of zero environmental footprint required that the company solve difficult problems in every aspect of the business, in the classic definition of problem solving: to make something undesirable go away. It required eliminating toxic materials throughout a supply chain, reducing overall energy use, driving costs out of what are inevitably more expensive processes if they are green ones, and driving bad habits and mind-sets out of seasoned manufacturing pros. To accomplish its never-before-attained goal, Interface developed a genius for problem solving.

Moreover, sustainability-minded companies approach problem solving differently from traditional ones. If they are serious, they identify and solve the root causes of problems rather than expeditiously making the symptoms go away.

Efficiency

Faster time to market beats competition.	Lower cost of production means more profit.	Take the easiest path. Remove barriers. Some things are easier not to know.	Pull out all stops to meet deadlines. Beat last year's or last quarter's numbers. Get to "Yes" as quickly as possible.
Waste is less important than speed. Don't worry about conserving materials if that slows things down.	Cheap materials matter more than safe or healthy ones. Fewer employees means less cost; squeeze the most from each of them.	Bullet points are a better alternative than transparent communications. Lobbying can be easier than compliance.	Start the cycle all over again. Continually drive for efficiency by reducing cost and increasing speed. Reward short-term results, not long-term vision.

Sustainability

A long-term vision for sustainability engenders loyalty and overcomes competition.	Profit and value are created simultaneously.	Dig deep into every aspect of the business; be willing to uncover unanticipated challenges.	Never take your eye off the ultimate purpose. Pivot as necessary to get there.
What materials and processes allow us to achieve the vision? What is the speed to market that can be achieved with that vision in mind?	How can a shared purpose drive better collaboration and productivity? How can profit and sustainability be built in?	How can we tap the power of limits to solve whatever challenges arise? How can we keep an open mind about all possibilities?	How can we continually build on what has been learned and accomplished? How can the past help us go further?

HOW TRADITIONAL BUSINESS PRIORITIES MILITATE AGAINST SOLVING ROOT PROBLEMS SUSTAINABLY

As a successful industrial corporation, Interface relies upon established manufacturing processes, with capital-intensive physical assets and an interdependent supply chain that reaches around the world. It is a public company with a board and shareholders who care what Wall Street thinks. Despite these pressures and responsibilities, the company recalibrated while moving forward. It transformed itself in a way that had never been imagined before, a vision that others considered impossible if they considered it at all. To do that, it engaged in both creating and problem solving: the former, to develop a new model for an industrial company, a new vision of what was possible; the latter, to remove barriers along the way.

But understanding Interface's current state requires returning to its past.

The transformation began in 1994. Frustrated because for someone who considered himself "customer focused," which meant being a step ahead of the people who bought his products in understanding what they need and want, Anderson was fielding an increasing number of questions he had never thought about and didn't have an answer for: "What are you doing about the environment?" they asked. He didn't know.

To rectify the situation, he called together an international group of Interface people who did. As they prepared for the discussion, the team told Anderson he should open the meeting with a presentation of his own environmental vision. Not surprisingly, he didn't have one. What happened next is what Anderson called "a spear in the chest experience." A copy of Paul Hawken's *The Ecology of Commerce*[3] "landed on his desk" and woke him up to the crimes of his industry and company. The pain that he felt in learning about his beloved company's role in environmental destruction began a ripple effect on Anderson, his company, his industry, and the world. This was the beginning of Interface's higher purpose. Like Josh Treuhaft in his quest to end food waste and Ruth Gates in her work to save coral reefs, Anderson found the real reason why his enterprise existed: to help save the planet instead of destroying it.

He laid out his environmental vision to the ad hoc task force on August 31, 1994. Called Mission Zero, Anderson's promise was to eliminate any negative impact the company had on the environment by 2020 by redesigning its products and processes, developing new technologies, and reducing waste and reliance on nonrenewable sources of energy. According to reports from the meeting, "reactions were mixed." A sales executive recalled, "Our first response was sympathy, because we all loved

Ray and it was quite clear that he had snapped under the pressure of running the company."[4] A CEO without instincts for social design might have dictated the new direction, presenting goals to his executive team and bringing in new people to shake things up if they didn't comply. Anderson engaged his organization, taking the time to get people excited about the vision no matter how crazy they considered it. Then he worked with them in developing a path that led from one experiment to another, learning along the way, using transparent communication and the power of the purpose to engage an ever greater network of willing participants.

Anderson was a persuasive leader whose voice had a deep, slow, Southern-accented cadence that sounded like a voice-over for messages from on high. While every CEO knows the importance communication plays in leadership, Anderson took on the role of chief proselytizer in his quest to engage his company, partners, board, and shareholders in what his audience thought at first was an impossible mission.

He became both poster child and muse for the sustainability movement, the go-to speaker whose face was projected on screens at industry and sustainability conferences, schools, and anywhere else he felt his story would move the effort forward. In the early years, that meant first explaining what sustainability was, describing its importance, and helping people understand the issues before he could lay out Interface's plans for acting on them. His energy was relentless, his passion contagious, and his courage inspiring. But his business success is what gave his vision its power.

Ray Anderson died on August 8, 2011. In his book *Confessions of a Radical Industrialist: Profits, People, Purpose—Doing Business by Respecting the Earth,*[5] he listed the company's accomplishments: greenhouse gas emissions had been cut by 82 percent, fossil fuel consumption by 60 percent, waste by 66 percent, and water use by 75 percent. Sales had increased by 66 percent, earnings had doubled, and profit margins had increased. Current statistics paint an even more impressive picture, with the company's carbon footprint continuing to decline.

It can be intimidating to look at what Interface has accomplished. It's easy to assume it required superhuman skill and lottery-winning good fortune. But the social design recipe is all here, and Anderson used it: a vision big enough to contain everyone's future and concrete enough to be actionable; a willingness to ask questions and not know the answers until they emerged from experiments; collaborative creativity in partnership with a network of suppliers; transparency and brilliant communication at every step.

Opposite: A fisherman from the Danajon Bank, the only double barrier reef in the Philippines, with one of the nylon fishing nets that destroys the marine ecosystem there. *(Interface/ZSL)*

Above: Community members collect, clean, and sort nets, matching high-level commercial standards. *(Interface/ZSL)*

Opposite: Interface and the Zoological Society of London helped establish community banks to help local residents manage and save the income they earn from collecting and selling nets. Shown here is a community bank meeting on the island of Sag in the Danajon Bank, Philippines. *(Interface/ZSL)*

Above: The finished product, in a room carpeted with Interface's Net Effect Collection, made with 100 percent recycled yarn. *(Interface/ZSL)*

Long before his passing, Anderson planted seeds for the even greater accomplishments unfolding today. In April 1997, for the company's twenty-fifth anniversary, he invited another international group to gather in Maui, this time expanding the circle to include Interface's important suppliers. It was clear that meeting the ambitious goals the company had set for itself would require its partners to sign up for the mission impossible as well. That is precisely what Anderson asked them to do: collaborative creativity in action.

In the words of one attendee at the gathering in Maui, the group was composed of "the most sustainable people and companies in the world." Yet even they said "This guy is crazy" as they left his speech and headed to the greens to play eighteen holes. While swinging and putting, they supported each other in their view that what Anderson wanted couldn't be done. Giulio Bonazzi, CEO of Aquafil, a supplier of nylon materials to Interface, took a different view. "He's crazy," he said to himself, "but he's expressing something very important." As it happened, Bonazzi's decision to stay put and think about Anderson's challenge was a far more profitable way to spend the day than playing golf. After thirteen years of effort, Aquafil succeeded in manufacturing 100 percent recycled nylon fiber, called ECONYL®, which, Bonazzi said, "we previously believed was technically and economically impossible." Aquafil has grown, in partnership with Interface, into one of the world's major suppliers of fiber, light-years ahead of competition, as it helps write a new history for sustainable manufacturing every day.

With a different cast of characters working in more places and touching larger ecosystems, Ray Anderson's values, his drive to realize the impossible, and his mastery of the principles of social design live on. Net-Works, one of Interface's new ventures, is moving beyond the vision for zero footprint to explore the social value that a manufacturing company can create. Net-Works purchases discarded fishing nets from residents of small coastal villages and transforms them into carpet tiles. For the first time, Interface has added poverty to the list of challenges it is shouldering.

In the words of Miriam Turner, who was Interface's innovations director in Europe, the Middle East, Africa, and India in 2012, the company is building "a 'relay race' mentality to innovation where we can pass and receive the baton to and from others."[6] Another of those invited to the Net-Works table was a friend of Turner's from college, Nick Hill, Conservation for Communities technical specialist at the Zoological Society of London (ZSL). Hill came with experience in working on environmental and livelihood issues in the Philippines. This uncommon collaboration brought together

Interface, the ZSL, Aquafil, and people in poor coastal communities in the Philippines and Cameroon. Innovations from social organizations, finance, conservation, technology, sourcing, and manufacturing have been integrated to create a new model for a manufacturing company with a restorative supply chain. The relay race of networked, collaborative creativity enabled this new partnership to solve both social and environmental challenges.

Discarded fishing nets are a dangerous and growing environmental problem for the most delicate ecosystems and poorest coastal communities. Crab-fishing nets, for example, typically last for only three to six months before the crabs poke holes in them, but they're made from materials that last for centuries (nylon 6, the same material used to manufacture carpet yarn). The damage they do to marine life and the environment is devastating, whether by trapping and killing tortoises and seabirds or transforming the landscape into a wasteland of fluffy white trash. In the Danajon Bank in the Philippines alone, the length of nets discarded each year, laid end to end, is equal to one and one-half times the circumference of the world.

In essence, Net-Works buys end-of-life fishing nets from residents of coastal communities, using a model that provides residents with an additional source of income and incentive to protect their environment; supplies material for Aquafil to turn into carpet yarn; and supplies Interface with fully recycled material for carpet tiles. One of its chief innovations is the development of community banks, a concept widely used and proven in development but rarely deployed in conservation. Since its inception in 2012, Net-Works has collected 142 tons of discarded fishing nets, given 1,500 families access to finances, and made it possible for 62,000 people to enjoy a healthier environment.

Creating this mutually beneficial new model required the solution of many problems along the way. For years, conservationists struggled to inspire local residents to preserve their marine ecosystems. But other priorities take precedence when people have almost nothing to live on and no access to finances or livelihood options. Community banks solve multiple problems by ensuring that the money earned stays local. They protect residents from loan sharks and help them learn financial management. For Interface, from a commercial perspective, the community banks became a single point of sale, reducing the collection costs of material spread over a wide geography. Local residents have found the opportunity to clean up their communities to be a compelling incentive, a chance to transition from life on a small, dirty island to one that instills pride and a sense of accomplishment in making it clean and beautiful again. Reflecting one of the principles of social design, it has changed their identity.

Big, fluffy nets are difficult to transport. An affordable bailer had to be designed, and it could not rely on electricity. "The technology was somewhere between a car jack and a wine press," the team says, and "shows the power of lateral thinking and the importance of holidays and wine." The baler has been baling nets without breaking since the project began.

Discarded nets collect unwanted materials that, if not removed, will contaminate the yarn during processing. A method was developed for stripping nets of organic materials, ropes, and weights before shipping, a time-intensive process requiring patience and care to ensure that Aquafil receives nothing but nylon 6 in the bales. The materials coming out of the Net-Works projects are now the highest-quality nets supplied from anywhere in the world.

Another problem was how to ensure that this new social and commercial venture had a business model that would deliver a return acceptable to the board of directors, meeting the needs of shareholders as well as the residents of tiny oceanfront villages who had never heard of Interface or considered carpeting their homes.

The approach that Interface and Net-Works mastered is one that every organization with a goal of real innovation can use: Make space for and devote energy to the process of creating, recognizing that it is a process different from problem solving. Make it an intentional effort, unencumbered by nagging concerns about how to get there. The power of the new vision will overcome whatever barriers may arise.

Interface has proven that it's possible to be successful without being destructive. In fact, it has demonstrated how manufacturing companies can actually generate social value. It's not easy. It requires creative leadership, a willingness to forge relationships with unusual partners and to question every accepted rule about how things are done. But the rewards for this kind of success are clearly there, in both financial and social measure, and the profit is shared by everyone on Earth.

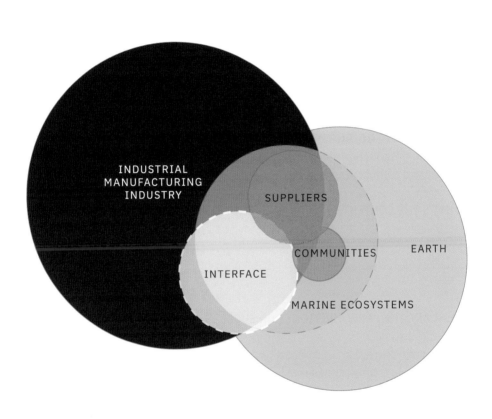

INDUSTRIAL
MANUFACTURING
INDUSTRY

SUPPLIERS

COMMUNITIES

EARTH

INTERFACE

MARINE ECOSYSTEMS

HOW INTERFACE AND NET-WORKS ANSWERED THE SOCIAL DESIGN PROCESS QUESTIONS

WHY ARE WE HERE, AND WHAT ARE WE TRYING TO DO?
Become a "mission zero" company and lead the way for others to follow. To use our strength and network to solve social problems as well.

WHAT'S THE CONTEXT?
Lots of problems. A global supply chain in a typically destructive industry touches every aspect of the planet and the people on it. Environmental issues are connected to social issues, such as the livelihood and well-being of communities where materials are sourced.

WHAT ARE THE PRECONDITIONS FOR SUCCESS, AND HOW WILL WE KNOW IT?
The technology needs to deliver. The business has to make sense financially and contribute to the mission. The product has to be of excellent quality; every aspect of production and technology needs to be proven and in place.

WHAT ACTIONS CAN WE TAKE TO GET THERE?
Engage a broad community of partners and ask them to do the impossible. Support and inspire the creative process with the time, resources, and intention it needs.

DOES IT WORK?
Measure its impact on environmental, social, and financial scales.

CHAPTER 9

Erik Hersman
Tapping the Power of Limits

TO TEST THE RUGGEDNESS OF THE RUGGED ROUTER HE WAS INTRODUCING to the frontier markets of the world, Erik Hersman traveled to the edge of Lake Turkana in northern Kenya—the world's largest permanent desert lake and one of the most remote and unforgiving places on the African continent. To test his conviction that despite the challenges of climate, infrastructure, and inexperience, Africa will be the next global source of technological innovation, he traveled to California's Silicon Valley.

Hersman likes challenges. He uses what others see as impossible limitations as inspiration. Time and time again, he has tapped the power of limits to create breakthrough products and platforms. His approach is easiest to track in his latest venture, BRCK, but is evident in each of his serial ventures. And adventures.

On March 3, 2017, Hersman sent an e-mail to his early-round investors with news of a journey he'd begun that day. Unlike many of the escapades he undertakes, this one did not include confronting bull elephants or fording turbulent African streams on a motorcycle. This ten-thousand-and-change-mile journey from his home in Nairobi entailed navigating the dangerous waters of Silicon Valley and

Seattle through conversations with Facebook, Google, and Microsoft—the bull elephants and turbulent streams for technology startups. This trip to California was a
quest for money and partnerships—conversations that put Hersman and BRCK at
the center of investigations into how to rethink current ideas about cloud comput-
ing. He was there to make the case for why the BRCK, the "homegrown" African
product after which his company was named, could overcome the barriers these
giants had encountered in their quest to connect critical, untapped markets to the
Internet and to their products and services. Even though these giant organizations
have almost unlimited resources and the best technologists in the world competing
for jobs, Hersman is convinced that despite his own limited resources, his connection to the real world on the ground in Africa's still unconnected places will make the
difference between success and failure. Because Hersman instinctively innovates by
collaborating with his network of friends and colleagues, he is able to achieve scale
far beyond his investment or the size of his organization.

The BRCK is a tough, versatile modem and router, designed with clear-eyed
attention to the needs of places with unreliable connectivity infrastructures and challenging conditions (such as heat and dust) that cause electronics to fail. With a battery
that lasts for ten hours, the BRCK and its progeny will withstand spikes of up to 400
volts and can be charged with anything from a solar panel to a car battery. It connects to the Internet via cellular network, Ethernet cable, or Wi-Fi network and will
automatically switch that up if the one in use goes down. A built-in global SIM card
connects to cellular networks in 140 countries and has forty gigabytes of storage and
its own Wi-Fi network that can accommodate twenty devices concurrently. Because it
is open-source, the BRCK can connect other devices, such as water pumps or weather
sensors, which can be managed easily by an interface on the cloud. All this functionality, which could be developed only with intimate knowledge of a place and its users,
is contained in an elegant black box roughly the size of the familiar building block from
which its name derives. The ingenious design of the product mirrors the flexibility and
resourcefulness of the company behind it. The BRCK is an invention born from, and in
service to, the limitations and challenges it's meant to overcome.

Hersman's vision for the BRCK is simple but outlandishly ambitious. He wants
everyone, even in the most remote rural villages, to participate in the education and
opportunities that connectivity provides. He wants to build the first billion-dollar African corporation and, in the process, to prove to the world that an African technology

company can not only catch up but lead. But the BRCK is just the latest in a series of breakthrough technologies and enterprises Hersman has designed, and there is much to be learned from his approach. He has managed to use the limitations of corruption, extreme climate, lack of infrastructure, and limited technology to do what most people without limitations can only imagine.

On global maps that use shades of blue to illustrate where innovation comes from, almost the entire continent of Africa, except for the pointy South African tip, is gray. Until very recently, Africa was a recipient of technological innovation, not a source. For most African countries, whatever is new has been imported: invented by people born elsewhere, designed to fill needs that exist somewhere else, adapted with varying degrees of success. In particular, Africa has not had the right mix of resources for innovations in hardware that require pristine, precise manufacturing facilities or access to suppliers of hundreds of different electronic components (or even a few), easy shipping and delivery of parts, or a pool of experienced engineers who know how to put them together. Add to all this a foundation of bureaucracy, corruption, and political instability, and it's easy to see why few have attempted what Hersman is doing. But then, few have Hersman's resourcefulness or his ability to see opportunities where others see problems, let alone engage a diverse community in taking them on. He is a natural leader who succeeds by creating with the people who share his understanding of the countries and contexts where he works and who also share his values.

Hersman's path reflects the influence of his evolution, from blogger and citizen journalist (@WhiteAfrican, Ushahidi) to geek participant and patron of the nascent tech scene in Africa (iHub) to founder of a business with a good shot at changing the continent's future (BRCK).

Hersman's parents were American missionaries, linguists who migrated to Africa, where they translated the Bible into the local Toposa dialect of South Sudan. The importance of communication, understanding, and connection was one of their son's early life lessons. Raised with traditional Christian values, he was taught to believe in what he calls "something bigger" than himself, which is reflected in the higher purpose of his enterprises, including BRCK. The protected comforts of his parents' home in America and the raw reality and exuberant natural beauty of Africa contributed radically different lenses to his worldview. He attended the Rift Valley Academy in Kenya and then Florida State University. The paradigm-shifting explosion of technology that took place in the 2000s, when he lived in the United States with his young family, provided a larger context for him to imagine what might also be possible for Africa, where technology was still an idea disconnected from daily life and entrepreneurship was rare. "Most people who grew up as children of missionaries don't go into business," he said. "I, however, had other ideas and from the age of eight I had turned over a wooden crate, cut a hole in it, and was selling gum on the mission station in Nairobi out of my mini kiosk."[1]

This double dose of culture, of being deeply immersed in two places and therefore more worldly than either one, gave Hersman a perspective held by few Africans and even fewer Americans. He knows each place better because he can see it through the eyes of the other. Like most Africans, he is impatient with people who define the continent by its problems and blindly accept the picture created through media of HIV/AIDS, famine, or civil war. Yet he knows from decades of living in Africa what the real challenges and barriers are, from daily disruptions of Internet connectivity to the larger, intractable dynamics of too little infrastructure and too much corruption. These kinds of pervasive challenges stop traditional "innovation from somewhere else" approaches in their tracks because they are invisible and unpredictable to anyone from the outside. They require an agile, systemic approach that works on root causes rather than symptoms and the invisible human dynamics that inevitably determine the success or failure of any enterprise, instead of only hardware and transactions.

LEARNING ON THE GROUND WITH A BAND OF BLOGGERS AND HACKERS

In 2004 and 2005, only a handful of bloggers were writing about Kenya, and all of them knew each other. In East Africa, the last major region to be hooked up to the rest of the world through fiber-optic networks, all Internet connections were routed through satellites, making them slow and inconstant at best. Bloggers served as on-the-ground journalists, covering events too small and local for reporters from regional foreign media to notice. The territory Hersman covered in writing for his *WhiteAfrican* and *AfriGadget* blogs reflected his passion for business, entrepreneurship, and technology. He turned every new invention, event, and enterprise he discovered into a story, scouring the country for evidence of Africa's tech potential so he could shine a light on it to help it grow. He wrote about funders and what they were funding and helped inventors connect to each other and become part of a larger community. He provided context for young inventors to see themselves as part of a larger global community. He championed an aspect of Kenya's identity the country didn't yet know it had, encouraging more people to believe in the potential of Africa and join in the transformation.

One of Hersman's frequent collaborators and fellow bloggers was Juliana Rotich. She was living in Chicago at the time, working in the data warehousing department at Sprint after studying computer science at the University of Missouri. During Kenya's 2007 elections, she was visiting her family in Eldoret, one of the most explosive spots in the country during the violent civil coup that erupted there. During her visit, when professional media outlets shut down and the airport closed, it was up to Rotich and other citizen journalists to take up the keyboard and report on what was really going on.

Another blogger and collaborator, Ory Okolloh, put out a request for help. She wanted to create a platform that would report the locations of incidents of violence as they happened. Hersman and American blogger David Kobia set up a site that mapped the incidents that Ory and the Kenyan blogger network reported to them. In June 2008, these four blogger-journalists transformed their site into an open-source mapping software platform called Ushahidi, meaning "witness" or "testimony" in Swahili. After it was deployed during the Kenyan elections, in January 2009 Al Jazeera used the platform to monitor violence in Gaza. Then, in 2010, when the earthquake struck Port-au-Prince, Haiti, Ushahidi was used by a volunteer army of technicians, members of the Haitian diaspora, and the U.S. Marines to locate and rescue survivors. (Rachel Brown, founder of Sisi ni Amani, profiled in chapter 12, was one of the volunteers and was moved to launch her own effort against violence.) Since its founding, Ushahidi has been deployed 120,000 times, seen 10 million posts or "testimonies," and reached 25 million people in critical situations.

BUILDING BRCK

From within the Ushahidi organization, BRCK began small, and personal, with a desire to solve the team's own issues with connectivity. Power outages and poor Internet connections had people changing locations during the day and hanging out in coffee shops and supermarkets just to keep working. Then, in October 2011, Hersman met Henk Kleynhans, founder of Skyrove, a company that manages the resale of Wi-Fi connectivity. When he talked to Kleynhans about his frustrations with connectivity, Hersman realized that no one was making routers to serve the African market. On a flight home from South Africa, he sketched the router he would make; then he

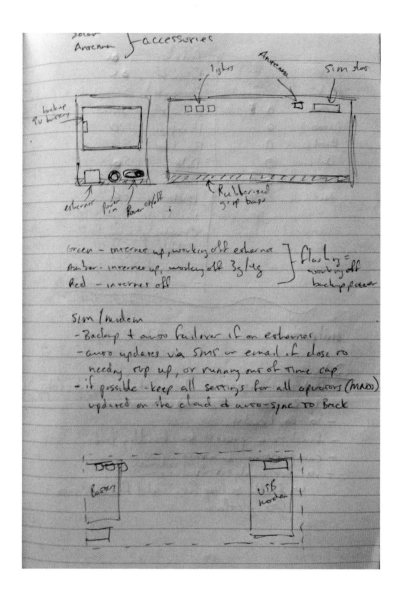

Opposite, top: The real thing: the BRCK, the basis of what Hersman hopes will be the first billion-dollar African tech manufacturing company. *(BRCK)*

Opposite, bottom: Stuck crossing the seasonal river on the way to the village of Korr in northern Kenya. *(BRCK)*

Above: Page from Erik Hersman's notebook with the original sketch of his rugged router concept.

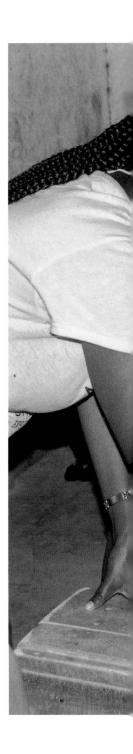

Top: The Dadaab Refugee Complex, about ninety kilometers (roughly fifty-six miles) from the Kenya-Somalia border, is the largest in the world, with almost a quarter of a million people. The UNHCR WASH project (United Nations High Commissioner for Refugees, Water Sanitation and Hygiene) needs to treat and pump a total of 10 million liters (nearly 3 million gallons) of water per day from twenty-eight boreholes scattered around the complex. To improve the process, BRCK and UNHCR teamed up to provide a solution that would enable remote monitoring of water generation and treatment using the PicoBRCK as an IoT (Internet of Things) platform.

Bottom: En route to Pemba Island, off the southern coast of Kenya. The final challenge on this leg of the Made in Kenya expedition took place at a notorious smuggling port on the island just before sunrise, with the heavy task of unloading all the cargo onto the beach by hand. *(BRCK)*

Right: Janet Maingi shows women from Kiltamani, Samburu, a new lesson on the Kio tablet, BRCK's product for revolutionizing classroom education. *(BRCK)*

presented the idea to the team to add all the features they'd like to see. The first prototype was completed in 2012.

The model for how Ushahidi and BRCK were invented reflects the process of social design. New endeavors begin with an urgent and ultraspecific need: in the case of Ushahidi, to witness the violence in order to name it, shine a light on it, and stop it— not in general but at specific places on the map during particular incidents. Each one involved someone with a unique voice and story to tell. In the case of BRCK, the need was to fix the unreliable connection to the Internet and make its opportunities available to people who have never been connected before. And so on, with iHub, where the need filled was an absence of a coworking space in which young inventors could collaborate. Whatever the end product, the impetus is need and lack, limits understood in specific terms. Because the challenges are framed concretely, they have power to provoke greater creativity than if they were abstract generalities. Because help is needed urgently and resources are scarce, they demand resourceful solutions using what is at hand. Thinking is not weighed down by expensive materials or restricted by established processes, nor is it complicated by outside experts who bring answers that worked somewhere else. It grows from the bottom up, from what is missing; it is a method in direct opposition to inventions developed in innovation labs that are protected from the real world within large institutions and then marketed, at great expense, to convince users that they have a need. In contrast, Hersman is essentially manufacturing opportunities for people who use his inventions to make them (and themselves) better.

Hersman and the vast number of people around the world who have collaborated, partnered, shared stories, and used his technologies and platforms provide concrete evidence of the invention and innovative thinking that limits can inspire. Their approach is a model for any other place where things are broken and missing.

ORGANIZATIONS ERIK HERSMAN HAS FOUNDED OR COFOUNDED

AfriGadget Blog, 2006

Hersman was a close follower of the African hardware scene; *AfriGadget* featured homebuilt electricity generators, vehicles, coolers for transporting camel's milk, biogas digesters, and clean cookstoves. He knew no one who was a specialist in networking and embedded electronics.

Ushahidi, 2008

Developed to map reports of violence in Kenya after the 2008 elections, Ushahidi is now a social enterprise providing open-source software and services to improve the bottom-up flow of information all over the world.

iHub, 2010

A coworking space for Nairobi's technology community, iHub offers the tech community a place to innovate with mentorship, business support services, access to start-up and product development workshops, and connections to potential venture funding and partners. Between 2010 and 2014, iHub gained more than 15,000 members; incubated 152 companies; spawned a consulting group, research arm, and user experience lab; and inspired at least six other tech hubs in Nairobi and many more across Africa via the AfriLabs network. It has attracted a growing group of international investors, venture capitalists, and donors, including the in-house based Savannah Fund, of which Hersman is a founding partner.

Savannah Fund, 2011

This seed capital fund specializes in early-stage high-growth technology investments in sub-Saharan Africa, with a goal of bridging the early-stage to venture capital investment gap.

BRCK, 2013

BRCK is a hardware and software manufacturer dedicated to connecting frontier markets to the Internet in three main areas: consumer connectivity, education, and enterprise Internet of Things.

Gearbox, 2015

The first major hardware maker-space in Africa, Gearbox is described on its website as "a space for people who design and make things."

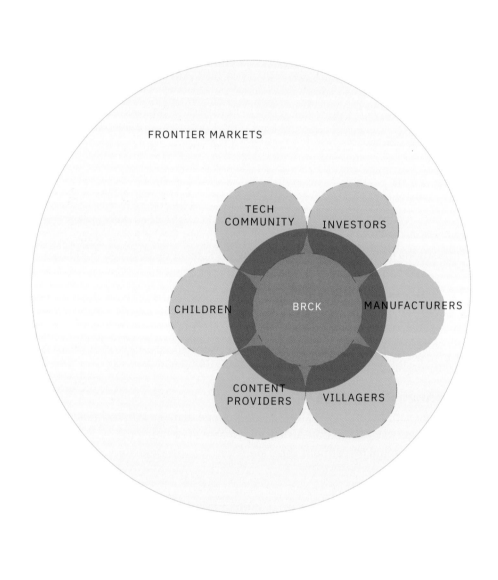

FRONTIER MARKETS

TECH COMMUNITY

INVESTORS

CHILDREN

BRCK

MANUFACTURERS

CONTENT PROVIDERS

VILLAGERS

HOW ERIK HERSMAN ANSWERED THE SOCIAL DESIGN PROCESS QUESTIONS

WHY ARE WE HERE, AND WHAT ARE WE TRYING TO DO?
Solve social problems at a scale large enough to reach the frontier markets of the world, using technology and entrepreneurship. Connect people in rural villages to opportunity and children to education.

WHAT'S THE CONTEXT?
Corruption at every level of government. Challenging weather, lack of markets and capital, and no manufacturing or technological infrastructure.

WHAT ARE THE PRECONDITIONS FOR SUCCESS, AND HOW WILL WE KNOW IT?
Products have to solve human needs and be affordable and desirable. Technology needs to work in all environments; connectivity has to be reliable.

WHAT ACTIONS CAN WE TAKE TO GET THERE?
Engage the global community of technologists, journalists, and makers. Find partners, work with what's on hand, invent what's not.

DOES IT WORK?
Do people use it? What did it change?

CHAPTER 10

Paul Polak
The Story Is in the Context

EIGHT HUNDRED MILLION PEOPLE IN INDIA LIVE IN RURAL VILLAGES. Two hundred sixty million people in East India lack access to safe drinking water. The water readily available to them is contaminated by fecal pathogens and is the single largest cause of illness and death among children, lost income and productivity for adults, and high costs of medical treatment. Most people live in hamlets of fewer than three hundred households, too small to be viable for current water companies to deliver to them.

To Paul Polak, this is a familiar challenge, one he has taken on before and won. It's a system of poverty and ill-health that he believes can be changed by the people who live within it if they're given the right tools. Ultimately, he sees it as an opening to convince big multinational corporations to follow him into these new markets, to make these people, who have never been treated like respected customers, part of the global economy and its benefits.

Polak is an eighty-four-year-old revolutionary and perhaps the most effective on-the-ground agent of change in the reduction of extreme poverty ever. He is a proponent of market creation and a living exemplar of what he calls "radical practicality," which he has put to use, so far, in helping more than 20 million small-acreage farmers in Africa and South Asia move from subsistence-level survival into the middle class.

In his world, his work is called "development," the label used by funders and big nongovernmental organizations (NGOs) whose mission is to eliminate poverty. Among development experts, Polak's ideas about market creation as the way to end poverty were initially controversial because they refute the theories upon which much development is built. He is vehemently and vocally against charity or any reliance on government subsidies or on NGOs that think they know best what poor people need. Instead, he believes in treating poor people like customers, granting them the same respect and agency that any other customer has, making the means available to them to build their own local economies and become independent. Like Jeffrey Brown, Polak is convinced that individuals have the ability, given the right tools and access, to change the conditions that have made them poor.

In 2005, Polak joined one hundred of the most influential designers from the United States at the Aspen Design Summit, convened to imagine the future of the profession. His reasons for showing up were, like his theories for solving poverty, simple and practical. When someone told Polak that what he was doing was design, he said he wanted to find out "if there was any truth to that." Because if there was, he had his own designs on the design profession—to turn it upside down. Ninety percent of all designers, he said, worked only for the 10 percent of the people in the world who have money. He wanted them to design for the 90 percent who have none. Polak had founded a global NGO dedicated to reducing poverty in Africa and South Asia (International Development Enterprises, now iDE) and had, against all odds and opinions, managed to sell more than a million treadle pumps (think StairMaster® without the electronics) to people who make less than two dollars per day. This simple bamboo construction allowed people to bring up groundwater and grow cash crops in the dry season, helping them earn enough money to educate their children and move into the middle class. He had founded other enterprises, too, selling "radically affordable" practical tools, such as cheap plastic drip irrigation systems, that helped people overcome mundane barriers to prosperity that other development experts overlooked. All of this earned Polak reverence among people who worked on eliminating poverty, but in no way had anyone considered what he was doing design. And among successful Western designers who live off fat commissions and have never even witnessed the extremities of poverty, let alone imagined working for clients who earn two dollars a day, his ideas were curious, to say the least.

In practice, Polak's approach is a good deal more complicated than it sounds because he goes to the trouble to include the poor people he wants to help in the process. His method and the results he's achieved underscore the importance of context in social design: of looking beyond the narrowly defined symptom to learn directly from the person about the dynamics of his or her life. He has interviewed more than three thousand two-dollar-a-day farmers, asking them why they're poor, and discovered that they inevitably know the answer. It is a method developed during his years as a research psychiatrist, based on the insight that there is always a larger social context in any human situation and that none but the people in the middle of it understand what the true context is.

PAUL POLAK IN CONTEXT

Although he works on complex issues, Polak has been guided by the ethos of "learning to do the simple and obvious." His work as a psychiatric researcher laid the groundwork for his radical business ventures. As a shrink, he questioned everything: what his peers' definition of mental health was (absence of symptoms) and how it compared with that of his patients ("when I have a job and a safe place to live"). He questioned why only some people with mental illness have the kinds of breakdowns that land them in hospitals, while others seem to manage okay. He wanted to interview people outside the sterile rooms of institutions so he could better understand what their lives were like, what dynamics affected them. He named that real-life outside context "social architecture." Within the social architecture of his patients' lives, Polak saw a causal relationship between mental health and poverty that, for him, made it impossible to treat one without addressing the other.

A turning point came when Polak followed Joe, a mentally ill, homeless man in Denver. Hanging out in Joe's three-foot-ceilinged sleeping quarters under a loading dock, following him to soup kitchens and storage lockers at the train station, Polak saw opportunities everywhere for entrepreneurial ventures that could help poor people in the city make money while providing them with needed services. One outcome of trailing along with Joe was the design of a patient-owned pharmacy, which opened the next year.

Years later, on a visit to South Asia with his wife's church, Polak was affected by the poverty he saw as well as the opportunity to test his learning at scale. The practice of talking with mental patients in their environments turned into days on end spent talking with poor farmers and their families, observing them in their homes and fields. He engaged them in conversation and respected their opinions instead of accepting traditional views of the causes for and antidotes to poverty. He had a deep-seated respect for the farmers based on his personal experience, too. He believed in their agency and understood they did not choose to be poor—did not want to be helpless recipients of charity. That ability to listen and understand people, and his entrepreneurial instincts, grew into a nose for viable business ideas in poor villages all over the world.

To traditionalists, whether in mental health or development, the patience required for Polak's level of observation can seem like a waste of time. What he has proven, in both fields, is that granular immersion in context pays off in success at a massive scale. His goal is to jump-start economies that will reach every one of the 767 million[1] people on Earth who make two dollars or less a day.

Paul Polak's father escaped to Canada from Czechoslovakia during World War II—saving his immediate family but failing to convince other relatives and friends to come along. Polak's message is that we shouldn't ignore what's happening in front of us: "All too many times in my life I have encountered people who make disastrous mistakes because they keep their eyes closed to what is happening around them. Each time, I remember what my father's friends and relatives said when he pleaded with them to escape. 'But what would we do with the furniture?'"

Looking at Polak's portfolio of enterprises at any one time can be confusing. At the time of this writing, for example, he is working on a plan for torrefaction (a process using heat to convert biomass into a coal-like material). He is converting mesquite, an invasive species, to make fuel that doesn't contribute to global warming, and he is making affordable solar-powered pumps to capture water for crops. While he is passionate and relentless about ending poverty, he remains agnostic about the way he solves problems to get there. Like Josh Treuhaft and Jeffrey Brown, Polak is constantly trying out new ideas and better ways to reach the goal, asking questions and recalibrating tactics on the basis of what he learns. This openness to innovation has allowed him to show less visionary companies that markets can be created where there are none, that poor people can be customers. His ultimate hope is that they will follow his lead, creating competitive markets and further driving innovation.

SPRING HEALTH

Polak said of his venture that delivers safe drinking water to rural villages in India: "Actually, I don't give a shit about water purification. I wanted to demonstrate that addressing global problems through a new frontier multinational structure that made money and didn't depend on the begging bowl was the most effective way of reaching scale." He had experience with drinking water through iDE and with irrigation. He wanted to see if he could sell safe water at a radically affordable price and deliver it to people living in places considered too far to reach. If he could prove that was possible, he thought, it would be a model for other organizations to participate, contributing to local economies.

He launched Spring Health in India because he knows the country well and had a team in place there. He knew the dynamics of the small rural villages because he'd visited so many of them. He knew the sickness and disease, had seen the children's suffering firsthand. These are the people with whom Paul has spent days on end: the people who inspire him.

Essentially, Spring Health is a water purification delivery system that supplies safe drinking water purified through electrochlorination—a proven technology that's affordable at the bottom of the pyramid because of its low capital and operating costs. A hub-and-spoke delivery model completes the "last fifty meter" supply chain, keeping operational costs low and enabling rapid expansion. The business model is high touch, high volume, and high margin, and it is scalable and replicable, with the ability to reach 200 million people.

Current details about Spring Health, which change continually, are that over 150,000 people (more than 30,000 households) in 260 villages receive safe drinking water from the company daily. Home delivery of clean water costs seven cents per day. Partnerships and incentive-based profit sharing have been established with local village shop owners and entrepreneurs. Capital expenditure, blitz marketing, and operating costs per village are roughly $2,000 per year. Each electrochlorination plant costs $250 to install and is capable of producing enough chlorine to sanitize 80,000 liters of water per day. The company has a staff of more than 60 employees and utilizes more than 300 deliverymen on a part-time basis. More than 230 village entrepreneur partners sell Spring Health purified water. Jobs are created for plumbers, masons, and electricians who provide supply chain support. Operations have begun in rural Odisha, India, with plans to scale up across the country in the coming years.

Getting to these numbers was a bumpy road with dangerous curves and dead ends, but Polak never lets failed experiments deter him. The first test in India was to find out whether people there had an interest in buying water in the first place. He raised $50,000 to conduct a research study, only to find out that the guy he hired to do it was "a skunk." "The whole beta test was a total waste of money," he says. "Turns out they recruited the shopkeepers, and paid them, filmed people carrying water to their homes. I got a touching picture of two little kids carrying water, hauling it from the shop to their home, but found out later they were hired by the guy I hired; they weren't buying water at all." That's not the first time something like this has happened to Polak, but he says, "If you don't have the motivation to steam past that kind of thing, you never get anywhere."

Polak applies hard-earned skepticism to new situations. When looking for an Indian firm to help with evaluation, he knew from past experience that small firms were better because the senior partners are more likely to do the work instead of passing it off to less seasoned workers. He met Jacob Mathew, cofounder of a large firm called Idiom Design and Consulting, at a conference. He shared his concern that with his small budget, a "flunky" would be assigned to him. Mathew surprised Polak by not only committing to personally work on his assignment but also accompanying him to a village in Odisha. His measure of a partner is how close they're willing to get to the customers and how many details they're willing to sweat. Mathew proved himself to Polak when he won the confidence of the villagers. They confided in him why no one would use a certain water tank. Some "untouchables" in the village had inadvertently touched the spigot. Nobody went there again until the shopkeeper blessed the tank, completely emptied it, and refilled it. On the other hand, Polak says, "Jacob thought I would be some fat-assed American who would never bother talking to people on the ground. Then he saw me joking and laughing with some village women. That's when we trusted each other."

Another thing they learned together in Odisha was that people didn't want to come to the kiosk to buy water. They wanted to pay extra and have it delivered to their homes. Seeing that as another business opportunity led Polak and Mathew to consider how to provide transportation. Successfully addressing this need required the calculations, trials, and adaptive thinking that are central to each one of Polak's enterprises.

Jacob Mathew designed a seven-dollar rack that could haul seven jerry cans[2] on a simple bicycle. That worked in the beginning, but close to a hundred jerry cans had to be sold in order to break even, so they looked for something that would carry more jerry cans at a time. A platform rickshaw pulled by a bike would haul thirty. There was concern that it would be too expensive, but it turned out to be an easy thing. Virtually every shopkeeper could afford a bicycle rickshaw: one and a half rupees for delivery multiplied by one hundred is enough to pay off a rickshaw if it's a used one. Shop owners realized they could use the rickshaw for a bunch of other things: they could haul kids to school in the morning and get paid a few pennies. Polak says, "We learned to our astonishment if you had a volume generator, it helped the shopkeeper into a new attractive source of income." Tests have now been done with motorized rickshaws, with unanticipated benefit because customers place a higher status on motorized rickshaws. And now the local leaders of Spring Health have decided to switch to twenty-liter jerry cans instead of ten-liter ones because they improve the efficiency of delivery. This kind of logistics analysis is expected from big commercial operations but is rarely considered for the needs of people who live in poverty. It makes all the difference in the world.

The lesson here again is that plans are useless because it's impossible to anticipate how things will work on the ground, how people will react and what will motivate them to participate. With every prototype, thinking evolves as needs demand. The motorized rickshaw handles a hundred jerry cans at a time, but to make it economically feasible takes three trips in a day. That poses the practical problem that three trips takes a lot of time driving on poor rural roads, making it impossible for the driver to stop at every home, because a lot of time is lost waiting for people to answer their doors. A hub-and-spoke model was developed, with five drop-off points in the villages.

Polak knows that despite the fact that you're selling something that will help people, even when it's what they say they need, there's no guarantee they'll buy it. That's why having a marketing strategy is a key component of any enterprise. Typically, the marketing campaigns are in a constant state of evolution. For Spring Health, two different marketing campaigns were tested. For the first one, people were hired to go door-to-door, offering to test the family's drinking water for free. The result was visual evidence of contamination—all sorts of wiggling things. Polak learned that young and older people react very differently to seeing the evidence. Young people find it disturbing and want to switch to clean water right away. The parents aren't always convinced. They say, "We've been drinking this water our whole lives, and look at us; we're fine."

The second marketing campaign involved hiring two separate theater troupes. Each one wrote a play and put on two performances a day in the villages. Because the performance takes place on the streets, people don't have to leave their homes to watch it. The plot is a bit unexpected. Even though health is a serious topic, people won't watch if there is no humor and music. In these plays, there is always a buffoon who says he doesn't need the clean water and refuses to drink it. The buffoon, of course, gets diarrhea and commences moaning and groaning in the middle of the play, even fouling his drawers.

In the end, the theater troupes were too expensive to use widely as a marketing device. But Polak is never deterred by the need to continuously adapt because it's just a part of the scaling process. Spring Health is currently implementing a price increase in Odisha, which will go toward delivering more products to homes. The cycle never ends. Something works for a while, and then it needs to be tweaked and adapted.

Plans are to expand from Odisha to Bihar, where different water technologies will be needed and, probably, different distribution strategies. Polak thinks all this is worth it in order to serve his customer base: every one of the people on the planet who live in rural villages and earn two dollars a day.

TRANSLATING THE SOCIAL DESIGN PROCESS FOR BUSINESS

To recast Paul Polak's approach to ending poverty through the new lens of "Paul's just a damn good businessman, and here's how he's done business in places where there was none," the following are his theories, proven by a lifetime of action and results.

1. Marketing 2.0

Typically, businesses don't like poverty; they see nothing in it for them, and they've been right. From a business standpoint, poverty has been a lousy investment: trillions of dollars spent, a temporary dent made. Most of what has been tried hasn't worked.

There is no question that selling products to people who make two dollars a day is a hard way to make a buck. But Polak is setting out to prove that when you know what you're doing, there's a multitrillion-dollar marketplace[3] waiting to be had—you just have to turn marketing on its head to see it.

Polak is a marketer of the most creative kind, commissioning Bollywood films to be screened on the sides of trucks and going door-to-door with demos showing people the bacteria in their own drinking water, scaring them into buying pure water. And, not least, understanding that an aspirational brand—part of every one of his businesses—plays the same role with poor people that it does with the fashionistas of the world.

2. Go for the Market Disruptors—in Poverty as in Business

When looking to create systemic transformation, identify the keystone, transformational products or services. They have a cascading effect, creating ripples of change and growth in other areas. For example, the chain reaction of Polak's torrefaction business: raise $25,000 to put up a torrefaction plant in a village, which creates products worth $600 per day, $180,000 per year. The plant represents jobs for four people, small-acreage farmers who then have money where there was none before. There are jobs as well for the people who pull, chop, and pile the mesquite that's burned, dry it, and deliver it to the plant—seven jobs for every village. This creates a wealthy enterprise and prestige for the town, which attracts more business. The torrefaction plant makes energy cheaper, helps all the businesses that use it to reduce costs and raise profits, and positively impacts climate change. All that transformation for a modest investment.

3. Even When You're off the Map, It's Location, Location, Location

Anyone who sells anything knows that you need to put yourself where your customers are. Sometimes that's on a high-traffic street or mall; sometimes it's in a place that's easy to find on the Internet.

To do business where Paul is doing it, the principle is equally inviolate, but the locations are wild. For example, for Spring Health, the water purification business now rolling out in India, *kirana* shops double as purification centers, adding clean water to the toothpaste, biscuits, and candy they typically sell. These humble kiosks in rural villages don't look like prime real estate for a big product launch, but they are centrally located, and they add up; there are anywhere from 6 to 9 million of them.

And it goes further, not just to the last mile but to the last fifty meters. Delivery men go door-to-door with water on the backs of motorcycles, and additional products are being developed to take advantage of that prime location on the back of the bike.

4. Never Take Your Eye off the Bottom Line

Whether you're dealing with millions or pennies, the discipline is the same: the numbers have to add up; the model has to make sense. There are no exceptions. Even though the numbers are small, it doesn't mean there aren't places to find efficiencies and make a profit.

Again, in the torrefaction business, by shortening the collection radius of biomass from fifty kilometers to four kilometers and switching from big machines to carts or tractors, a 40 percent reduction in cost can be realized, the basis of what can become a huge business.

It scales well beyond the village. When people move from $2 a day to $3 or $4, they become consumers; that makes a huge impact on the global economy. They start to pay taxes; they have smaller families. Raising the income of farmers has been proven to raise the economies of entire countries, such as China, South Korea, and Taiwan.

5. Think Huge, and Don't Be a Victim of Your Emotions

Polak's rule is that a business has to have the potential to reach 100 million people and generate at least $10 billion in sales in order to be worthwhile. Seeing that potential will make it real.

While passion and empathy draw people to help others, they are anything but the secret to success. Hardheaded business strategy will go much further to change lives. Caring deeply about helping people should spur pragmatism, not romanticism.

There are practical lessons here for all involved: don't fall in love with your altruism when you don't have a sustainable solution to poverty, and don't fall in love with your new business idea unless it can really impact the world.

Opposite: A customer in the village of Gopalpur in Odisha, India, waits for the morning delivery with her collection card in hand. *(Pragya Mahendru)*

Page 158: The rural countryside in Banki, in the state where Paul Polak takes on the challenge of last-mile delivery. *(Pragya Mahendru)*

Page 159: Spring Health trucks must maneuver narrow village roads to deliver clean water to their customers. This is the village of Jatinwa Gaon in Odisha, India. *(Pragya Mahendru)*

Opposite

Top: A Spring Health deliveryman fills blue jerry cans with clean water in Tangi, Odisha, India. *(Pragya Mahendru)*

Bottom: A typical well that supplies groundwater in Tangi, Odisha, India. This is the drinking water supply for many families. *(Pragya Mahendru)*

Above: The Spring Health truck is ready to deliver jerry cans containing clean water to customers' door-steps in Tangi, Odisha, India. *(Pragya Mahendru)*

$2/DAY FARMERS AND THEIR FAMILIES WITH-OUT SAFE WATER

PURIFIER

RETAILERS, DELIVERERS, MARKETERS

CUSTOMERS

HOW PAUL POLAK AND SPRING HEALTH ANSWERED THE SOCIAL DESIGN PROCESS QUESTIONS

WHY ARE WE HERE, AND WHAT ARE WE TRYING TO DO?
Demonstrate that addressing global problems through a new frontier multinational structure that makes money and doesn't depend on the begging bowl is the most effective way of reaching scale.

WHAT'S THE CONTEXT?
Two hundred sixty million rural people in East India lack access to safe drinking water. What's available is contaminated by fecal pathogens and is the single largest cause of illness. Most people live in hamlets of fewer than three hundred households, making them too small to be served by current water companies.

WHAT ARE THE PRECONDITIONS FOR SUCCESS, AND HOW WILL WE KNOW IT?
The last fifty-meter delivery gap is solved. An economy is jump-started that benefits the entire village and, eventually, everyone who used to earn two dollars a day.

WHAT ACTIONS CAN WE TAKE TO GET THERE?
Start the chain reaction and monitor every step. Test various marketing schemes; monitor use in one village; then expand to others.

DOES IT WORK?
Did multinationals enter these markets to continue the momentum begun by Spring Health?

THE POLAK RECIPE[4]

Achieving the simple and obvious is never as easy as it sounds. To effect any-thing at a systems level, especially to create the kind of transformational change that will grow an economy and help people move from poverty to the middle class, requires a complex and interwoven strategy based on specifics of place, culture, and human, financial, and natural resources. Polak's plans almost always include an invention—a gadget of some kind or another using technology that is simple enough to be radically affordable for the people who are expected to buy it, such as the treadle pump for bringing up groundwater that Polak first developed, or a cheap rubber hose. It's not important that they be new technol-ogies, but it is essential that they've been proven to work in similar conditions. A tight plan is developed for how the domino effect will start with the use of the gadget and continue to the creation of jobs and income for entire communities. Not least, there is always an "aspirational brand" and marketing plan, as with any other target customer group, since making something available and afford-able to people is not enough to convince them to buy it.

For anyone wishing to replicate Polak's approach, there are a number of nonsubstitutable ingredients and inviolate principles:

- Spend sufficient time (days and weeks, not hours) on the ground with the people you want to help in order to see the world from their perspective. Spend time in their homes, in their fields, with their families.
- Ask about their aspirations, their worries, their opinions about the problems they face, and what they think the solutions are. Weight their opinions at least as heavily as your own.
- Keep an open mind. Do not impose your own views.
- Look for the social architecture as well as the physical realities.
- Take stock of the resources available to them: their own labor, local flora and fauna, water, and existing infrastructures or systems that could be co-opted for distribution or market flow.
- See if there are challenges waiting to be turned into opportunities. Invasive species, for one example, can become a resource.
- Look at everything with an entrepreneurial mind.
- Be cheap. Practice working with what exists rather than deciding there is not enough. Tap the power of limits.

- Make sure your idea can start a chain reaction and become a keystone intervention that will lead to other changes throughout the local system.
- Make sure that whatever you're selling is affordable, not just by Western standards, but accessible to the people who you expect to buy it. Even twenty dollars is a huge investment when you have to work for ten days to earn it.
- Remember that people won't change their habits just because you're convinced it's good for them.
- Design an aspirational brand, and be prepared to develop and adapt a full marketing campaign to convince people to do what you might think is already painfully obvious.[5]
- Do the math, not just for the profit margins on your product but for the whole chain reaction you hope to spark in the form of a revitalized economy.
- Find some money to get started, but keep your eyes open to the fact that most people with money won't understand what you're doing because the ideas are not sexy enough for traditional investors and not charitable enough for grant makers.
- Create a working model.
- Hire local people; pay them fairly; give them ownership of the company.
- Be on the ground constantly to see how people react to your idea.
- Be prepared to pivot and constantly evolve the idea as it rolls out. Nothing works in real life the way it seems it will on paper, and people's behavior is unpredictable.
- Do your best to be ready for the upending events that happen in poor places: droughts, floods, and other natural disasters, political upheaval, war.
- Do not, under any circumstances, allow anything or anyone to dilute your relentless determination to persist in your efforts or to compromise your belief in the possibility of sustainable change.

To test your recipe before you head off to serve it, see if it satisfies Polak's "Why bother?" trilogy. If not, toss it out and start again.

1. If you haven't talked to at least twenty-five of your customers,
2. If it won't pay for itself in the first year, and
3. If it can't reach a million people, don't bother.

CHAPTER 11

The Buffalo Niagara Medical Campus

Using Networks to Create a New Future for a City

MIRACLES, BIG AND SMALL, ARE MUNDANE on a medical campus. Hearts are mended, brains rewired, rashes soothed, wounds healed, and diseases cured. Miracles are harder to come by in the forgotten neighborhoods of America, where lives and days are made of the stuff that breaks hearts and opens wounds.

Buffalo, New York, ranks third in the country for the number of people living below the poverty line. For the residents of its poor neighborhoods, that means no jobs, high crime, and very little access to healthy food. Like most American Rust Belt cities, its downtown had been abandoned by those who could afford to leave it and move to the suburbs for better schools, invisible violence, and more segregated living.

The Buffalo Niagara Medical Campus spreads its miracles far beyond the edges of its own property, using its financial strength to improve the economy of the city, using its understanding of health to make its neighbors healthier. It also uses the principles of social design to develop relationships and programs that create more opportunities for Buffalo.

By the numbers, the bustling campus spans 120 acres of real estate in the city. Sixteen thousand people occupy almost 9 million square feet of clinical, research, education, and office space in 9 member institutions and 150 private companies and nonprofits. Every year, 1.5 million patients and visitors come from all over the city, surrounding states, and across the globe in pursuit of better health.

In 2002, the medical institutions on campus formed a nonprofit named, somewhat confusingly, BNMC. The mission of this new organization was fairly modest: to facilitate collaboration among the occupying institutions and maximize the potential of the campus to contribute to the city. No one imagined, until they proved it, what a difference they could make. And no one believed, until they saw it, how the power of networks and collaboration could be harnessed in service to the city's health. Today, the evidence is plain: BNMC has created jobs and improved transportation, education, food access, entrepreneurship, and energy.

BNMC is an "anchor institution": an organization, typically medical, educational, or government (meds, eds, and feds), with permanent ties to a location and the capacity to contribute to it as an employer, real estate developer, buyer of local services and supplies, and attraction for related businesses and knowledge workers to locate in the city. Creating an anchor institution is a strategy for city revitalization that's been in practice for more than seventy-five years and is measured, for the most part, in economic terms.

What makes BNMC unique as an anchor is that instead of defining its objectives on the basis of its own institutional needs and what its operations can contribute, the organization has created a vision and goals based on the needs of the communities around it. An example of the typical approach is to say "We have ten job openings; why don't we look for local people to fill them?" or "We spend hundreds of thousands of dollars on laundry; could we find a company in the city instead of contracting with a national firm?" Instead, BNMC applies the principles of social design by collaborating and cocreating. It invites neighbors into the conversation, asking them what's important to them and then incorporating that into the plan. The first approach shifts some processes and resources around but doesn't affect the social architecture. The other requires creativity and a willingness to restructure the organization and purpose in response to what the community asks for and cares about. The people who stand to benefit from either of these approaches are likely thinking about the struggles in their lives, which ten more jobs and a more robust local laundry business cannot begin to solve.

BNMC has created more than 3,000 new jobs so far and built an innovation center that currently houses seventy-five start-up companies. Dozens of other programs have been developed that benefit not only the campus but also the people who live nearby. The collaboration includes everyone—ministers across the street and national politicians; the mayor of Buffalo and the governor of New York; small local start-up enterprises and a British multinational utility company; local activist groups and national foundations. So far, BNMC has attracted $1.4 billion in investments to the city and put the money toward new facilities that increase access to healthy food, clean energy, transportation, business innovation, and education. All of BNMC's activities are bundled into an approach called MutualCity: a new vision for a city based on mutuality and benefit for all.

Residents in the Fruit Belt, a neighborhood across the street from the campus, have solar panels on their homes, which were made possible through a special program developed for them by National Grid. Local middle and high school students attend the entrepreneurial boot camp on campus. Mobile garden and market sites brought 10,000 pounds of produce to food deserts last year. Street lighting is better, school lunches are healthier, and more corner stores sell fresh food instead of racks of Twinkie-like processed food products. Internships, job access, résumé writing, and mentoring are available. A Green Team of local residents have maintenance and landscaping jobs on campus, and residents can win scholarships to a coworking space. Employees have access to bike sharing, Zipcar rentals, and subsidized transit passes.

"GOOD LUCK; THAT WILL NEVER HAPPEN"

What makes the BNMC story more useful in mining for lessons to apply in other places is that it has accomplished all this in a city with more than its fair share of skepticism. Residents are tired of being famous for nothing but snowstorms and chicken wings. Any talk of change and new initiatives can scratch the scab off a not-so-deeply-buried wound called the Peace Bridge. This involved a painful and ultimately fruitless attempt to upgrade the bridge over the Niagara River that connects the United States and Canada via Buffalo. It became so contentious that the *New York Times* called it a "border war."[1] After nearly a decade of public dissension, plans to rebuild this symbol of friendship devolved into an ugly and irreconcilable political fight over whether to demolish the old bridge and replace it or build a new, adjacent one. For Buffalonians, the futile bridge plans became one more piece of evidence that their city "just couldn't get things done."

It wasn't always so, and perhaps it is the glory of the city's past that can make the present so painful: the structural reminders of the once vital industry that, in its prime, made Buffalo home to more millionaires than any other city in the United States. Buffalo was an important center for the abolition movement and a terminus for the Underground Railroad. It was called the City of Light for its innovation and early adoption of electricity, and it was part of the automobile revolution when the Pierce-Arrow Motor Car Company was in full swing. In an earlier century, Buffalo was the principal port for the massive volumes of cargo headed to the great American West to build the infrastructure and feed growth there. A drive through downtown Buffalo is quieter now, emptier. But there are reminders of its former glorious culture in the architecture by Frank Lloyd Wright, Eero Saarinen, and Louis Sullivan and the necklace of emerald parks designed by Frederick Law Olmsted.

Through its success, BNMC has helped change Buffalo's opinion about itself back to a city with a promising future. It has energized residents, local businesses, and a group of local funders and investors to engage with their city in ways they had not done in many years and has created unexpected creative partnerships.

It takes a city to turn itself around, and the number of people and organizations that have contributed to Buffalo's turnaround is so great that a map of engaged collaborators becomes almost as dense as a map of the city itself. But the vision, the orchestration, and the day-to-day efforts to continually push the boundaries of what BNMC can accomplish are led by Matt Enstice, the organization's president and CEO since its founding.

Enstice still comes across as the easygoing, well-mannered jock next door he was while growing up in Buffalo, the one everybody wants to hang with, who always has time for his friends and is inevitably the one who takes the lead in putting a game together. He is also a big thinker, a broadly curious natural learner, and a keen observer of human nature and social dynamics. Two experiences in particular illustrate the lessons he learned that have helped him become a social designer: one a brilliant success, the other an abject failure.

LEARNING FROM SUCCESS AND FAILURE, FRIENDS, FRENEMIES, AND FOES

After college, Enstice worked on Lorne Michaels's production team on *Saturday Night Live*. What he took away from his job there, in addition to the skills required for navigating enormous egos and still "getting stuff done," was the way "really random parts"—the myriad details of costumes and sets, individual skits, punch lines, and people—came together every week to make something much greater than all its parts: a show that, through Michaels's satirical vision, changed the country's discourse, invading its culture and redefining what we knew as comedy and television itself. That idea, of seemingly random small parts that, with the right vision, have the potential for game-changing influence, has shaped Enstice's work in powerful ways. It taught him the importance of a clear and compelling purpose and the need for collaboration and cocreation in attaining it. Perhaps most important, it showed him the role he wanted to play: the facilitator, or conductor, of a network of amazing partners working together toward something in which they believe.

The other lesson came from observing the Peace Bridge process as it unfolded. Listening to the endless arguments over which bridge design was the right one and who should make the decision, Enstice observed that the flaws were in the process, not the decision itself, that it was a bunch of politicians and bureaucrats squaring off with no way to have a productive conversation because of their truculent egos and irreconcilable agendas. He also observed that the process was one of exclusion, a peeing contest for power between the people who already had it. He said, "I believe if people in the community had been asked, even if they didn't build the damn bridge, they would have been fine as long as their voice was heard."

These two lessons came together to form a working methodology for Enstice. First, managing random, seemingly disconnected parts can result in disruptive transformation if it's done in service to a shared vision. Second, that process is strategy; the simple act of bringing people together to listen and be heard changes them, and through it, the journey to better conditions is begun. When Buffalo mayor Tony Masiello said, in 2002, "Why don't we have a medical campus?" he put his former chief of staff on the case, who lured Enstice back to Buffalo to work with him. Three months later, when the former chief of staff moved to Atlanta, Georgia, Enstice took over as leader of the fledgling BNMC organization with help from Tom Beecher, a wise and respected community

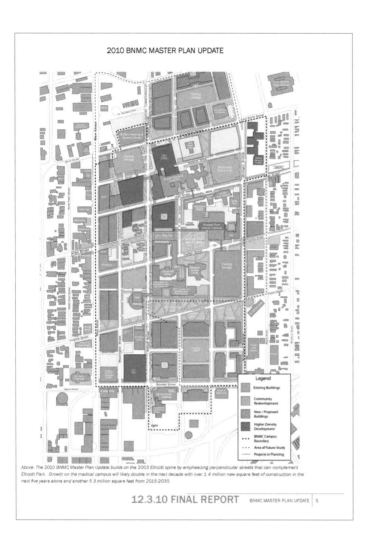

2010 BNMC MASTER PLAN UPDATE

Above: The 2010 BNMC Master Plan Update builds on the 2003 Ellicott spine by emphasizing perpendicular streets that can complement Ellicott Park. Growth on the medical campus will likely double in the next decade with over 1.4 million new square feet of construction in the next five years alone and another 5.3 million square feet from 2015-2030.

12.3.10 FINAL REPORT   BNMC MASTER PLAN UPDATE | 5

Above: The original plan for the BNMC campus, titled "Four Neighborhoods, One Community," integrated the surrounding neighborhoods in its vision for revitalization. Adjacent neighborhoods include Allentown, the Fruit Belt, and downtown Buffalo.

Right: An aerial photograph shows the campus in the context of its neighbors and the rest of the city, with Lake Erie in the background. *(BNMC)*

volunteer. They encountered, full on, the brunt of Buffalo's skepticism and self-doubt. That's when Enstice got to put what he had learned into action.

BNMC's first funder had also learned the benefits of collaboration and played a leading role in setting the conditions for its success. The John R. Oishei Foundation asked BNMC and its members to create a model that would show people how to collaborate, and it told them they would receive funding only if they did. That changed what had been independent and sometimes competing medical institutions into partners in envisioning what the medical campus could be. As a result, Enstice and his partners were able to "create a single voice" for the campus-sized community and hit the ground raising money.

Building on this foundation of collaboration, the lessons from the Peace Bridge and *Saturday Night Live* were integrated into what became the standard way of working. Volatile politicians, naysayers, and potential troublemakers were invited to the table—all those for whom an invitation to help make decisions "inside the tent" was the only way to prevent them from shooting at it from the outside. Enstice also included community leaders from the surrounding neighborhoods in the conversation and invited two of them to join his board of directors. It was a clear signal of his values and of his conviction that the project would fail if it didn't seek out and respect all the people who would either make it a success or help it fail. Since those early days, BNMC has refined its social design process into a standard practice for taking on new, more ambitious goals.

As the process unfolded, the same lessons proved invaluable again and again. Time itself provided another important lesson: that a goal as ambitious as making a city healthier requires years, not months, of dedicated, relentless, intentional effort. For a few years, there were monthly meetings with CEOs in which everyone would agree about what needed to be accomplished. All good, no problem, until Enstice and his team tried to follow up with their next-in-line commanders to actually get things

Opposite

Top: The adjacent Allentown neighborhood hosts the Allen West Art Festival every June. This two-day juried festival draws thousands of art lovers from around the country. *(Allentown Association)*

Center: BNMC established a bike-sharing program on campus to help employees get around the city without adding to congestion or carbon dioxide emissions. This photograph was taken on the annual Bike to Work Day, intended to convince more people to use bikes rather than cars. *(Khari Imagery)*

Bottom: During conversations with the community, seniors at a neighboring care center said they wanted to garden. The BNMC team built raised planters so they could do so without bending too much or kneeling. *(BNMC)*

done. Instead of the CEO's approval automatically starting the work in motion, what he heard was "That's not my job, and I'm not going to do it." Whether it was as simple as creating campus signage or adding parking spaces or as complicated as building a new facility or developing adjoining neighborhoods, no matter how vigorously heads had nodded approval in the meetings, nothing happened. Just as with the Peace Bridge, the answer was to hold meetings that included the chief operating officers, address the issues that only they saw, since they were the ones who had to do things, and let them go back to their CEOs for permission to get the jobs done. Other tweaks to the process came the same way, by comparing the number of feel-good decisions made in meetings with what was actually happening on the ground.

Talking to "anybody who would listen to us," Enstice said, yielded other lessons along the way. From Father Vincent Cooke, head of Canisius College: "You're going to run into a lot of resistance. When you do, don't fight it; move on to something else and those people will come around." This advice was translated into permission not to spend time trying to bulldoze through brick walls or to convince the die-hard opposers to believe. BNMC adapted, looking for places where progress could be demonstrated more easily, creating evidence that would attract the formerly skeptical to get on board.

A successful businessman suggested that BNMC "do what I did and steal shamelessly. There are a lot of good business ideas out there, and you don't need to reinvent the wheel." This began a pattern of creating unusual and unexpected partnerships that helped BNMC overcome the limitations of a small staff while adding the capabilities that new collaborators brought. When you are determined to be inclusive and a city is your purview, there is room to partner with just about any legitimate organization or individual who comes along. Designers of solar-powered streetlights became partners. A company selling eco-friendly hospital supplies became a business partner rather than just a vendor. Architects from the State University of New York's University at Buffalo became collaborators in an incubator and coworking space where BNMC mentors residents and neighbors.

When everyone is seen as a potential participant, relationships become generative instead of transactional. That is a critical lesson for anyone who wants to create any kind of lasting change. The list of BNMC partners includes the biggest names in government, philanthropy, business, technology, and entrepreneurship at the national, state, city, and street levels.

Through cocreation with diverse partners inside the city and beyond, BNMC is now in the middle of another redefinition, enlarging the circle of influence and impact. Partnerships that at first provided practical components of healthy medical campuses and neighborhoods have expanded to include Silicon Valley companies and international coding services in a new effort to make Buffalo a center of technology again. In conversations with local banks and businesses, Enstice uncovered a common problem—the challenge of attracting top tech talent in a single organization is difficult because the opportunities for creativity aren't there. He thought about all the people he had met who wanted to move back to Buffalo for the lifestyle but couldn't find the jobs they wanted there, and that gave him the idea to launch a center for coders and programmers. It will house a community of the best talent and will outsource work to local businesses. That is the kind of innovation that comes from collaboration and paying attention to the power of relationships. It's the social design process applied to a city, available to any other place or organization willing to invest the time and commitment to make it happen.

"Good luck; that will never happen" is not something Matt Enstice hears anymore. People from other cities come to Buffalo to learn the secret of BNMC's success. The history, the deals, and the people and organizations involved are a complex story worth careful study. But the real secret, available to everyone but difficult to do, is to lead through humility, define an irresistible North Star, and invite everyone who wants to come into the tent to create together.

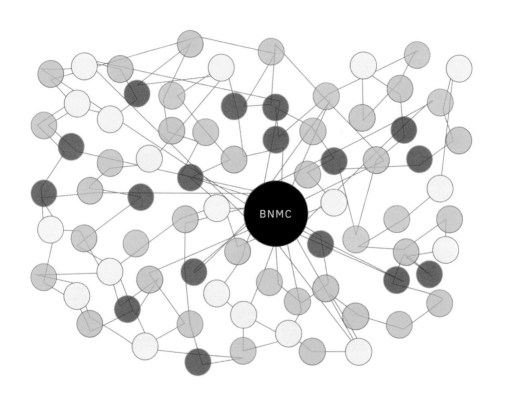

HOW BNMC ANSWERED THE SOCIAL DESIGN PROCESS QUESTIONS

WHY ARE WE HERE, AND WHAT ARE WE TRYING TO DO?

Use our resources and influence to invite anyone who wants to contribute to collabo-rate in making Buffalo a healthier city in every way.

WHAT'S THE CONTEXT?

Third-"highest" ranking in the country for people living below the poverty line. World-class medical center in the middle of it. Stakeholders include everyone from national and state politicians to the minister next door.

WHAT ARE THE PRECONDITIONS FOR SUCCESS, AND HOW WILL WE KNOW IT?

People at every level will participate and contribute. Things will actually get done. Businesses and former residents will move back to Buffalo.

WHAT ACTIONS CAN WE TAKE TO GET THERE?

Convene, network, forge partnerships, prototype, connect, promote.

DOES IT WORK?

What is the lasting impact? Did it start a ripple effect?

CHAPTER 12

Sisi ni Amani
Communicating the Way to Nonviolence

IN 2008 AND 2009, the sudden eruption of tribal violence during the elections in Kenya rocked the country, pitting neighbors against each other, killing more than 1,000 people, and displacing as many as 500,000 more. One year later, in 2010, Rachel Brown graduated from Tufts University with a bachelor of arts degree in international relations and founded an organization called Sisi ni Amani in Nairobi. She had been to Kenya the year before as part of a studies abroad program. She went back because she thought there was a chance she could help prevent a repetition of that election violence in the next national election, scheduled for 2013. She hoped to increase Kenyan citizens' engagement with the way their country is run and help them understand it better. "Sisi ni amani" means "we are peace" in Kiswahili. Like Josh Treuhaft, Rachel Brown was compelled by a passion she could not ignore to fix a problem far beyond the scope of anything she had ever contemplated. And Brown, like Treuhaft, carved her own path without a formal plan in place, by using real-time learning from communities in Kenya. By enlisting their participation and scaling up one step at a time, she was able to create a calibrated, relevant, and ultimately successful program. With help from thousands of new collaborators, through a ripple effect that spread like a peace virus from friend to friend and village to village, she succeeded, despite her youth and relative inexperience, relying on insights from people on the ground and large-scale community organizing.

While still in school, she had been struck by an op-ed she read in the *Boston Globe*.[1] The author said that Kenya's violence wasn't caused by tribal hatred, as was being reported, but instead was the fault of poor leadership and political corruption. The source of violence was power plays from an elite group of troublemakers outside the government. That theory was congruent with what she herself observed while studying in Nairobi: "There was so much organizing at the local level, and so much positive response." She found local residents to be engaged in the election and looking for ways to make the situation better. It made sense to her that forces from outside these communities were taking advantage, fomenting discord, seeding misinformation and fear.

A friend from school knew the humanitarian technology expert Patrick Meier, who had completed his doctorate at the Fletcher School of Law and Diplomacy at Tufts University and at the time was working with Ushahidi (see Erik Hersman, chapter 9). On January 12, 2010, when the earthquake hit Haiti, Meier immediately launched a live crisis map[2] on the Ushahidi platform. (His description of Ushahidi is "a multimedia inbox connected to a live map.") By midnight on January 13, Meier had found a dozen Haitians tweeting live from Port-au-Prince, "describing scenes of devastation but also hope." Within a day or two, the influx of messages from Haiti overwhelmed his small team, so he asked for volunteers to help, teaching more than a hundred students in Boston how to monitor media and map content. According to one of the participants, "Graduate students were running in and out of the Fletcher dormitory stamping snow off their shoes, sitting down in a crowded living room, and melting into the virtual world of their laptops. We were overwhelmed by the scale of work and the immediacy of need. It felt impossible to leave. One person would be ordering pizza, another fielding a request from the World Food Programme, and yet another talking to the media—but mostly, we sat in silence reading media reports and text messages from Haiti; struggling to find exact geo-coordinates of addresses on maps that had no street names."[3] Rachel Brown was among this group of volunteers, helping to record what grew to more than 2,000 individual reports during the almost nine days of the rescue mission. She was also learning how personal technology could be, how a neutral platform made from digital code could record individual stories and save the lives of the people who told them.

On the basis of insights from the *Globe* article, her own observations of enthusiasm and hopeful attitudes in Nairobi, and her experience using Ushahidi, Brown decided to return after graduation, determined to profile the different positive things happening on the ground in Kenya. She wanted to show an alternative narrative to the one being told, capturing stories in real time. Her initial idea was to map peace instead of violence. It is a testament to her instincts as a social designer that she left that first concept behind when conversations with communities revealed a different approach.

There are more than 30 million phone subscribers in Kenya, in a population of roughly 46.5 million. It was clear from the start that phones had been the weapon of choice in inciting the postelection violence, although Brown didn't know that until her local collaborators told her after their first public event. Messages like "While you were sleeping, rigging [of the election] was taking place" were used to build anger and create suspicion. Text messages were used to spread hate speech or to plan attacks on people from different tribes. Brown was hopeful that the same communication medium used to incite violence could stop it.

She began her social design process in the only way possible when you don't know where to begin. She asked questions, and she used what she learned to understand the dynamics on the ground. She used each new connection to guide her to the next. Answers to questions also revealed shared values throughout the villages. Each person she met became a part of the community. Somebody connected her to an activist in an informal settlement in Nairobi; he introduced her to ten different local youth groups there. She asked everyone where they would begin the mapping quest if they were her, and how they would go about it.

The advice she got was to begin by recruiting youth groups from each of the neighborhoods in Baba Dogo, the informal settlement, or slum, in Nairobi. Each neighborhood has its own identity, and until the neighborhoods were approached to join this new peace movement, they had never had an incentive to collaborate, only to compete. Local leaders decided that the first event should be a parade, and each invited the youth in their neighborhood. The result was a parade of about 120 new collaborators who marched on a path mapped through each neighborhood by the youth who lived there, with music, T-shirts, and signs that said "Text this number about peace." When they agreed to have a peace concert at the end, they all mobilized artists and musicians from their neighborhoods because they wanted to "make the story about peace as loud as the one about violence."

A story from that first event illustrates how Sisi ni Amani took hold. Brown says she didn't know what she was doing, but she trusted the people she was working with. When the decision was made to make T-shirts, one of the men had a way to do it. He costed it out, and Brown paid him what was an unusually large amount up front. Much later, reflecting on how Sisi ni Amani came to be, the man told Brown he'd been shocked that she just gave him the money. He said it wasn't usual for people to come in and trust local groups. Brown says, "Maybe the level of trust I had could be considered naive, but I think it's what made Sisi ni Amani possible. When trust was broken, we talked about it—when our expectations didn't match or we miscommunicated, we talked about it. We all came from really different backgrounds—so sometimes we'd understand things differently, have different expectations, and that could be challenging. But we fundamentally all knew we were in it together."

When that first parade day was done, Brown wrote it off as a failure because they got only a few text messages for all the effort they put out that day. All the others who marched, though, were excited. When she asked them why, they told her they had already known about each other but never had reason to come together. They also saw exciting proof that mobile phones and text messaging could be used to spread peace and not just violence. Brown knew she didn't have the answer, but she became committed to staying to help find one. Her willingness to see what was there instead of what she expected was a key reason for her success throughout the project.

After the Baba Dogo parade, other neighborhood leaders came forward to say, "You need to come here now. Where is our parade?" A few members of her team, who "knew NGO speak," said, "We need to do a strategic plan." Brown earned a bit of money from a consulting gig and hired a facilitator who, she thought, would help them sort out a plan.

An off-site strategic planning meeting was held in Narok, attended by people from Baba Dogo and Korogocho. The facilitator spent the first day and a half trying to coax answers out of them about the root causes of violence. It was a conversation that most of the people there had had before. The energy and excitement that had emerged from the parade was being dulled by conversations that were too abstract to be meaningful. Participants got frustrated, and Brown got frustrated because no useful or actionable ideas were emerging. On a hunch, she started mapping out the passes of a soccer game on a flip chart.

"The causes of violence are an everyday part of life here," she said, "but why did it erupt at the time and in the way it did?"

She began to diagram a mock soccer game with Team Peace and Team Violence.

"Who won the first pass?"

"Violence."

"Why?"

"They spread rumors; they lied."

"Who won the next pass, and what did they do? And what would we do to push back on the violence?

What was Team Peace doing?"

"Nothing."

Brown said, "As we did the analysis, they talked about how the rumors spread (first they were whispered; then, for example, on a market day, when people came together, they'd spread faster). The conversation became nuanced and detailed. I asked after each pass what Team Peace had done to play defense or turn it around; often the answer (until the very end) was 'Nothing' or 'Not much.' When I asked, 'What could have stopped this pass from being successful?,' we went back through it and started to imagine what we could actually do."

Suddenly the conversation moved from the theoretical to the practical. It helped people shift from abstract, disconnected ideas to specific things they could do. Rachel's pivot away from abstract jargon to a more practical framework, in response to what engaged her collaborators, produced the foundational ideas that would become Sisi ni Amani. Every one of them emerged from this single strategy session and mock soccer match.

Her team of organizers were now fully committed and had the beginnings of a strategy for action. They held another event in Kamukuni, refining what they learned from their first prototype: reaching out to additional activist groups and making direct requests for people to sign up with their phone number. The response was enthusiastic. Two thousand people registered in one day. That was also the day Brown's new Kenyan friends convinced her to ride a camel from one slum to another. They found it hilarious, she says. "The kids were flipping out; they thought it was the craziest thing they'd ever seen." For the expanding community of activists who wanted to work with Brown, this was a symbol of her commitment to them. They placed their trust in her to help them carry out a new vision. They had invested their own social capital in her, and she felt the weight of responsibility for what she had begun. This rapidly multiplying group of collaborators believed she would help them reduce the impact of violence during the next election. She thought she'd be in Kenya for the next six months or so. She was there for a total of four years.

It was "a ragtag group," says Brown, that continued to hold rallies and impromptu gatherings. At first, they used whatever they had on hand, writing names and phone numbers on scraps of paper and then typing them into a database one by one. With pressure to connect and enlist enough people to sustain momentum until the next election, events were pulled together in Baba Dogo, Narok, Mulot, Korogocho, Kasarani, and Nairobi. SMS surveys were used to learn what issues people cared about most, such as ethnic tensions, disagreements over land, and government corruption. According to Human Rights Watch in 2008, "No Kenyan government has yet made a good-faith effort to address long simmering grievances over land that have persisted since independence. High-ranking politicians who have been consistently implicated in organizing political violence since the 1990s have never been brought to book and continue to operate with impunity. Widespread failures of governance are at the core of the explosive anger exposed in the wake of the election fraud."[4] Other issues were unemployment, security, environmental issues, and police reform.

THE SISI NI AMANI TIMELINE

July 2010: Arrive in Kenya with the idea of peace mapping; meet some local peace activists from Baba Dogo.

August 2010: The first parade in Baba Dogo.

December 2010: Strategic planning retreat, followed by the Korogocho event, with the new idea of asking people for their mobile phone numbers.

2011: Grant from USAID/OTI. More than 7,000 subscribers sign up and receive civic education. Hire a program manager, which helps create an organization.

2012: Support from PopTech allows additional scale-up, plus improvement of the tech platform by the Praekelt Foundation.

November 2012: Major funding from USAID/OTI for a big scale-up; expansion to additional areas of the country.

March 2013: The election.

Not all villages were affected by the same issues, and a critical component of the success of Sisi ni Amani was that whether in person at peace parades or via text, messages were customized and hyperlocal, relevant to their audience and based on needs they had expressed. New partners joined continually, and experiments with different formats and content were always in the works. A theater group put on a play about rumor formation; a local radio program played the debates and texted subscribers to listen in, asking them to send questions about voting, laws and regulations, or rumors they were hearing. Brown's group used local teams to monitor hot spots where violence was more likely, and then they communicated with people in those areas continually. The team was constantly learning about people's concerns and questions by listening to everyone, everywhere. Brown's core group piloted a debate program and then launched it in new neighborhoods, sometimes with discussions that responded directly to recent local incidents. Forums on land education alerted people to the practice of "double leasing," in which the same land was leased to people from two different tribes. Other long-standing tensions over corruption and inequality were addressed by disseminating facts and being transparent about what was known. The goal, as Brown says, was "to empower communities with the information they needed and reduce their vulnerability to rumors."

In addition to the work in the streets and villages, Brown was writing grant proposals for funding to enable access to more sophisticated technology. In 2012, Sisi ni Amani received a grant from the U.S. Agency for International Development's Office of Transition Initiatives (USAID/OTI). The team was able to update the platform and add enough participants to begin going door-to-door. Seven thousand additional subscribers joined in less than two months' time. Everywhere they went, team members enlisted new leaders from local communities who could translate information on the issues they wanted to know about. And everyone who wanted to participate in the quest for peace signed on to receive text messages and spread the word to their friends and family.

In a social network that spread like wildfire, every day people met someone who connected them to someone, who introduced them to somebody else. Many people were known activists and had networks of their own. Some, such as a Maasai named Freddy Kamakei, came with experience in mediating and building peace. A lawyer joined who could speak to the legalities of land disputes; community leaders who understood policy signed on. With each new individual and network that joined, Sisi ni

Amani became both larger and more local. The platform and the mission of peace was a constant, but relevant information and language could be finely tuned to specific issues and places. The model for scale-up was to recruit teams and work with them to develop outreach plans for their neighborhoods. Whether it was rural Ololulunga or Sotik, Sogoo or Sagamian, every area required unique tactics, all different from the tactics used in dense informal settlements in Nairobi.

Team members were committed to spreading only truth, researching answers and confirming their accuracy with the Independent Electoral and Boundaries Commission. T-shirts made the peace-building army more visible, giving it an identity and a source of pride. Stickers for businesses declared their commitment to peace when posted in a window. A butcher in a small town in the Rift Valley noticed that people who came into his shop had begun separating by tribes and speaking in mother tongue. He asked for a packet of Sisi ni Amani stickers so he could make his position known by declaring his butcher shop a place of peace and encourage other shops to do the same. These visual symbols of belief and belonging may seem at first like frivolities, but they are important semiotics in any movement. They act as signals to others and create a sense of unity and belonging. Borrowing from the role that uniforms have played in peacekeeping throughout history, these simple T-shirts and stickers fulfilled the same need.

Many people on the growing Sisi ni Amani team had never had a full-time job before. Some were former inciters of violence themselves. Sisi ni Amani gave them a purpose, a way to channel their emotions into something positive. They were transformed by Sisi ni Amani's efforts and made its peace mission their own. It showed in the care they took with content: "Hey, this comma is in the wrong place. Fix it!"

The urgency of the looming election, and the need to reach critical mass in time, drove Brown's efforts to enlist larger partners who could help scale their text-based communications. February 2013 became a tipping point when Safaricom signed on as a partner, donating 50 million SMSs for the election period. These were used to increase the reach and frequency of the texts. PopTech, an organization in Camden, Maine, chose Brown as one of its Social Innovation Fellows and formed a larger working group that included the antiviolence group CeaseFire in Chicago, the South African mobile technology company Praekelt.org, and the global advertising agency Ogilvy & Mather. Finally, the resources to scale up were in place. In the six months before the election, 35,000 subscribers were added and fifty activist groups had joined the movement, each one feeding the specific information people wanted back to their individual villages. As the election approached, communication escalated daily. Because it was both networked and decentralized, with a hub-and-spoke model that generated many of the messages locally, content and timing were highly customized. The messages' relevance to what was happening on a given day, with a particular group of people, made them powerful.

Here's an example from November 19, 2012:

> Today we have reached out to our community in Mathare with messages of peace—we have sent SMS in English and Swahili to over 3,500 community members encouraging peace. We hope you will join us in passing these messages along as we also work on messaging for Kamukunji on Tuesday:
>
> ENG: Sisi watu wa Eastlands let us never blame the actions of a few on an entire community. Lets not bring bad effects of violence, let us maintain peace. . . .
>
> SWA: Sisi watu wa Eastlands tusilaumu kijiji mzima kwa matendo maovu

Images of the peace builders, on the streets or at rallies like the one in Baba Dogo, are filled with music, dancing, and joy. Sisi ni Amani brought hope and a sense of belonging that erased lines of tribes, age, gender, and power. It is difficult to fathom, without understanding how it happened, that one young, newly graduated white woman was the catalyst for such enormous change, for the hope and coordinated action and ultimate accomplishments of so many disparate people. In hindsight, the principles of social design that Brown employed are clear—learning from the people most affected, making small experiments and changing direction as needed, working with people's own identity as a source of strength, and using communication as an act of empowerment and inclusion.

Brown never thought she had all the answers. Of her time in Kenya, she says, "I saw a bunch of organizations with foreign founders who thought they knew everything. I didn't want to be like that. I tried to provide a platform for Kenyans to express their own desires to prevent violence." Like Paul Polak learning from his audience of rural

Pages 190–191

Sisi ni Amani staff and community volunteers march through an informal settlement in Nairobi during one of their first campaigns to enlist new subscribers to their SMS peace messaging platform. *(Sisi ni Amani)*

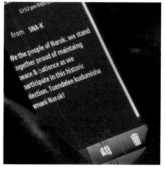

Above: A Sisi ni Amani organizer subscribes a local resident to the SMS platform. *(Sisi ni Amani)*

Right: A test SMS is checked for accuracy and clarity before being sent to targeted communities during Kenya's 2013 elections. *(Kenny Dalsheimer, from the documentary film* Peace in Our Pockets*)*

Sisi ni Amani organizers worked constantly in the Nairobi informal settlements to show people how to subscribe to the peace messaging service. *(Kenny Dalsheimer, from the documentary film* Peace in Our Pockets*)*

farmers, who knew exactly what they needed to work their way out of poverty, Brown met people who understood their own communities with clarity and had ideas for how to prevent violence but no resources.

The Sisi ni Amani representatives built social capital by walking around communities every day, going to markets, celebrations, funerals. "We placed a premium on supporting their social capital," Brown says. "I was giving them control, and I was willing to let people fail and learn. My team was going to mess up in ways I wouldn't, but I would have messed up worse because I didn't understand the community."

That granular knowledge allowed Sisi ni Amani to send messages that interrupted tensions and violence on the ground. "As hostilities arose leading up to the elections, we sent messages about unity. When rumors started to spread, we sent messages warning individuals against misinformation and urging them not to be manipulated. And when antagonism and small-scale skirmishes erupted, we sent messages about the consequences of violence and the need to prevent its escalation." Because the text messages were so finely targeted and timely, some recipients thought they were being watched, and so they held back from violence. They thought twice before doing something they might regret. Others thought the texts were a sign from God because there was no return number, and the message was so often the right one at the right time. Because the communications were calming, giving people an appreciation for positive action, they gave the impression that "someone is running the show," which in itself brought peace. Because messages indicated the names of places they were sent to, like the Nyanza–Rift Valley border, with its issues of cattle rustling, people in many small places were comforted by the fact that they had not been forgotten: "At least someone remembers us."

In total, more than sixty activist groups in seven targeted hot spots across the country were enlisted, and more than 65,000 people subscribed. All subscribers received customized text messages that addressed their fears and questions. The Sisi ni Amani campaign increased the number of Kenyans who went to the polls to vote peacefully, and, according to a study by the University of Pennsylvania,[5] it played a significant role in preventing another outbreak of violence.

After the election, there was tension while people waited to hear the petition on the results. Sisi ni Amani teams in Nairobi held forums so that people who supported both parties could come together at a time of high tensions. People had stopped shopping in shops owned by members of other tribes in some of these areas. "After the petition results and finalization of election results," Brown says, "we continued our work, turning political debates into accountability forums."

The story of Rachel Brown and Sisi ni Amani illustrates multiple social design principles. Small prototypes worked here because no plan could ever have anticipated the way the movement would unfold or what would be needed at a given place and time. Brown came to the project conditioned to think that the way to approach her goal was to write a detailed plan and apply for money to implement it. Because en-thusiasm and demand for rallies escalated so quickly, her team needed to work on the fly just to get going. In retrospect, this was the only approach that would have allowed them to respond to need and to test ideas for which they subsequently found funding. The obvious principle at play in Sisi ni Amani is the role that communication plays in addressing social challenges. Communication is how community is built, how hope is instigated and kept alive. More than anything else, in the case of Sisi ni Amani, communication built trust: between collaborators and among citizens. This open, cus-tomized, patient approach to communication is difficult for traditional organizations to adopt. It goes against old corporate structures, in which information is withheld to protect power. But Sisi ni Amani proved that its grassroots, networked approach to collaboration accomplished near-miraculous results at one of the most fraught, divi-sive moments in the history of Kenya. It is not difficult to list the many other places where these same results are needed.

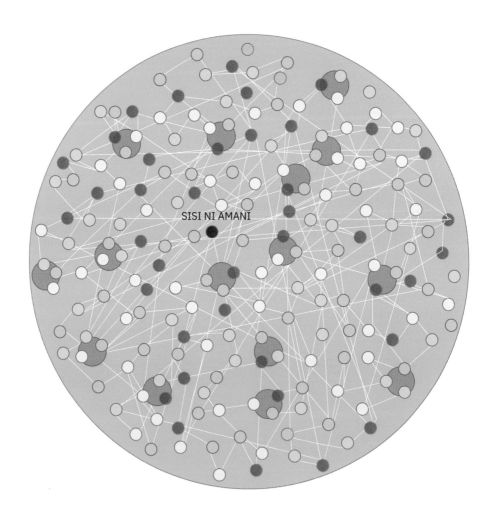

HOW SISI NI AMANI ANSWERED THE SOCIAL DESIGN PROCESS QUESTIONS

WHY ARE WE HERE, AND WHAT ARE WE TRYING TO DO?
Create peace in Kenya.

WHAT'S THE CONTEXT?
A history of violence fomented by a campaign of text messages. Factions that want to incite violence; disparate communities and villages that speak different languages and have different questions and concerns.

WHAT ARE THE PRECONDITIONS FOR SUCCESS, AND HOW WILL WE KNOW IT?
People have to choose to participate. Trust must be earned with truth. The right information needs to get to the places where violence might break out and stop it. The platform needs to be both mass and personal.

WHAT ACTIONS CAN WE TAKE TO GET THERE?
Engage people and build a team composed of people from all the villages who can connect and translate.

DOES IT WORK?
Was peace achieved? Did people vote? Was there lasting change in the way people treated each other?

CHAPTER 13

MASS Design Group
Process Is Strategy

MICHAEL MURPHY LOOKS THE PART of a successful, Harvard-trained architect. He is tall and carefully groomed, thoughtful and articulate. He runs a bustling design office with lots of architectural character in Boston's Back Bay, a stone's throw from the city's iconic Public Garden. He doesn't have a Boston accent, but his speech is careful and somewhat formally structured, almost like a building in which he carefully orchestrates which door, to which room, he will open next.

Beneath the controlled exterior is a relentless passion to revolutionize the purpose and process of architecture, to disrupt its hegemony of privilege and aesthetics. Murphy is redesigning the practice of architecture to include social value as well as physical beauty, and he has become one of the most visible and respected architects in the world by eschewing the time-honored architect-as-genius-hero meme.

MASS Design Group, the firm he cofounded with Alan Ricks in 2008, has seventy-five employees who work in more than twelve countries. There is an office in Kigali, Rwanda, in addition to the one in Boston. The company won the 2017 Cooper Hewitt National Design Award for Architecture Design, one of a recent string of prizes and recognition from *Fast*

Company, Metropolis, and *Contract* magazines and the Museum of Modern Art, to name a few. Young architects compete for jobs at MASS. The company has designed hospitals, tuberculosis clinics, and maternity waiting villages, where women from remote villages have access to reliable prenatal care not available in their home villages. The scope of the company's work has expanded, from health care to primary schools and a memorial to all the people in America who have been lynched. Every project is created for people who have never entered such beautifully designed environments, let alone had them designed with their needs in mind. Just as Paul Polak and Jeffrey Brown built successful businesses by treating poor people as valued customers, MASS succeeds by putting the rewards of the inhabitants of its buildings before its own.

MASS architects work to address the social consequences of built environments and what they consider to be the damage that architecture has done in the course of its history. Murphy believes that designers need to rethink the process by which buildings are conceived and built. Through a mission-driven social approach to design as well as a technical one, MASS avoids perpetuating the dysfunctional social dynamics of structures that dictate oppressive and unhealthy relationships among the people who live in them.

The first project to bring attention to MASS Design was the Butaro District Hospital in the Northern Province of Rwanda. In their approach to the assignment, the team questioned everything: Why does a hospital ward have to follow traditional layouts, with patients lying with their heads at the exterior wall while doctors and visitors have views out the windows behind them? What happens when sick people have a view out to the countryside instead of staring at other sick people all day long? Why are traditional designs for ventilation employed when they depend on a power grid that often fails, exposing patients to an airborne soup of diseases that linger and make them sicker than they were when they entered the hospital? Why are workers and materials imported from other places when people nearby need jobs and when local materials are more affordable and less energy is wasted shipping them in? Why are generic international designs that produce nondescript buildings used when traditional designs are more appropriate to the place and far more beautiful? To answer these questions, they didn't fall back on the old models of design, in which the experts decide what's best for untrained and unsophisticated people. They collaborated with Paul Farmer and his organization Partners in Health to understand the physical and emotional needs of patients and doctors. And, like Rachel Brown, Paul Polak, and

Jeffrey Brown, they collaborated with, and found inspiration from, local artisans and villagers, who had a deeper connection to their place, its needs and its traditions, than any outside professional ever could.

The answers they received inspired them to reimagine the role a building can play in the health of its inhabitants. Butaro is proof of how much a hospital can contribute to the well-being of a whole community, long before any patients are treated there. It embodies their goal to "employ, educate, and empower the local community,"[1] making everyone healthier. It is an illustration of how a system of natural ventilation can be designed, using only local breezes and open windows, that decreases infection rates. And how, by simply turning beds around, a ward can send patients home faster because they have a view of nature outside. How a building, instead of reinforcing the inequality of the sick and the healthy, can work to heal and restore.

Murphy devotes a good deal of time to wrestling with the dark history of architecture. He has used what he considers its greatest crimes as inspiration for ways to change it. He recognizes the unspoken assumptions and invisible dynamics of the profession, the rules and boundaries that prevent it from becoming more socially and environmentally conscious. He observes the ways of working that have become automatic and then reimagines how, with a higher purpose, they might be changed or replaced. Like Ruth Gates pushing the boundaries of scientific research to integrate social design, Michael Murphy is breaking the rules of architecture to include social value.

Before he became an architect, Murphy studied English literature at the University of Chicago (Renaissance poetry, to be precise). He still writes, as a way to investigate his own opinions about architecture's past and future and as a way to bring transparency to issues that have never been spoken or questioned. He challenges assumptions about why designers' needs always take precedence over users' needs, why power is only for the already powerful. He struggles with architecture's history of violence, aggression, and arrogance and does not trust its intentions.

Murphy writes about the structures in which people are their most helpless, such as hospitals and clinics, and how they dictate and then enforce the asymmetric relationship between caregiver and patient. He illustrates sample hospital floor plans from 1400 to today, with names like "cross-ward," "manor," "modern," and "block," to show how protocols and prescribed interactions adopted by the profession as a whole can take shape inside a single designer's head, avoiding the inconvenience—and missing out on the benefit—of talking with a single patient who might be treated there.

Pages 202–203: Construction of the Butaro District Hospital engaged local workers and utilized traditional methods and materials. *(MASS Design Group)*

Top: The Butaro District Hospital, in Burera District, Rwanda, opened in 2011. *(Iwan Baan)*

Bottom: The interior of the Butaro District Hospital reflects the design's intention to reduce the transmission of airborne disease by including natural cross-ventilation. *(Iwan Baan)*

Top: The Cholera Treatment Center, on the main campus of Haitian health-care provider GHESKIO, was designed to treat diarrheal diseases in response to the cholera epidemic that emerged following the 2010 earthquake. *(Iwan Baan)*

Bottom: The perforated steel facade of the Cholera Treatment Center was inspired by advanced technology and crafted by local metalworkers. It was custom designed to provide adequate sunlight and airflow. *(Iwan Baan)*

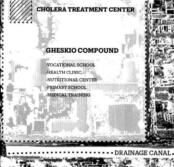

POST-EARTHQUAKE
TENT CAMP

BOULEVARD HARRY TRUMAN

CHOLERA TREATMENT CENTER

GHESKIO COMPOUND

-VOCATIONAL SCHOOL
-HEALTH CLINIC
-NUTRITIONAL CENTER
-PRIMARY SCHOOL
-MEDICAL TRAINING

DRAINAGE CANAL

Page 206: An annotated aerial view of Port-au-Prince, Haiti, shows the GHESKIO Cholera Treatment Center's location in the context of residents' extreme poverty. Decades of political instability and economic insecurity have left 60 percent of the city's 3 million people living in slums, with toilets, if they exist, rarely connected to sewers. Waste finds its way into drainage canals, spreading disease and compromising sanitation. *(MASS Design Group)*

Page 207: The GHESKIO Cholera Treatment Center is located across the street from Cité de Dieu, an informal settlement built atop a landfill. *(Iwan Baan)*

Public housing is nothing more than prison with a different name, Murphy argues, with poverty and segregation as its wardens. Massive towers in threes and fours and sixes are built to separate the poor from the rich and keep the poor in their places. They are carefully designed and developed not for the benefit or protection of the people who live there but for all the lucky others who, because of their privilege, will never have to. This is where architecture has committed some of its biggest crimes—in offenses disguised as public service. It is architecture as a series of experiments in all the ways to stack people on top of each other, hiding them away after their neighborhoods and trees and gardens have been torn down. Dark hallways; small, boxlike apartments with low ceilings and small windows; the mechanical repetition of hundreds of doors off identical corridors with bad ventilation and dirty carpets infused with the smell of last week's cooking. Like hospitals, these "homes" speak to their designers' cleverness, achieved without ever speaking to the future occupants.

But the work of the MASS Design Group does more than point out the flaws in current thinking. It illustrates a way to reinvent the practice to be more just.

GHESKIO CHOLERA TREATMENT CENTER, PORT-AU-PRINCE, HAITI

GHESKIO was the first permanent cholera treatment center in Haiti, built in response to the 2010 earthquake, which killed more than 220,000 people and left more than 1.5 million others homeless. The devastation of the earthquake exposed the shortcomings of a city built of structures so poorly constructed that when they literally fell over on people and killed them, no one was surprised. The earthquake also uncovered the frailties in the health-care infrastructure, which could not begin to accommodate those in need. Three million people live in Port-au-Prince, 60 percent of them in slums. Canals built by the U.S. Army Corps of Engineers in the 1950s collect rainwater and refuse and then carve tributaries through the city that distribute their toxins to residents before dumping them into the Caribbean Sea.

GHESKIO, a nonprofit based in Haiti that has been delivering care for HIV/AIDS patients since 1982, was MASS Design Group's collaborator on the treatment center. The organization's involvement with the Haitian government provided the contacts needed to work effectively with local bureaucracies and the context required to understand the needs of earthquake survivors and communities on the ground.

Architects around the world sent schemes for rebuilding the city and putting up emergency housing for survivors, crisis-mode templates for residences that suited the architects and builders more than their intended occupants. They followed architecture's traditional impetus to bring solutions in from outside, without an understanding of how people in Port-au-Prince wanted to live. This is evidence of what Murphy calls "disciplinary amnesia." Lots of designs were sent for temporary buildings and pre-made houses shipped in flat packages, along with other proposals to move people into shipping containers. Some ideas did address the lack of materials in a country suddenly without transportation or shipping infrastructure after the earthquake. In Murphy's mind, though, all of the submitted ideas forced decisions to be made for expediency, not the well-being of the people they were meant to help.

Another industry trend, for all-local fabrication, has become "overfetishized," according to Murphy, "as if the local is hegemonic." These two popular options—for prefab buildings shipped in from somewhere else and for those made entirely of local materials and construction—make the process of designing and building the primary concern. What's missing from the discussions is the question of cultural and human impact.

MASS Design asks questions that put social justice and the needs of the community first. What is the best outcome for people who come here for medical help and their families, and how can the design best provide that? What kinds of talent, materials, and resources exist in the community, and how can this construction provide value? How might the design improve the local environment, and what other services could it provide? In claiming the agency to question, MASS defines a new, inclusive, collaborative power structure for the profession.

For example, MASS designers believe that architects have extricated themselves from a building's functions, that they leave all that responsibility to engineers. To remedy that, instead of concealing the functional systems in the clinic, they decided to reveal them as part of the strategy: engineering function as an intrinsic component of design. Water, heat, ventilation, and power impact the occupants' experience with a building as much as the structure itself does. In making those parts of the building visible, MASS takes responsibility for the experience of the building's users, not just the structure's aesthetics.

Materials were hard to come by after the earthquake, but importing them denied work to local laborers. In the end, MASS subverted the market by constructing with indigenous technologies: earthen blocks made from local soil. Local artisans and village laborers built the clinic, in an intentional program that rotated villages and engaged women and minorities. A women's cooperative woodshop staffed by current and former sex workers solved the problem of how to source local furniture. Working together, the women produced beautiful furniture and upended the idea that custom construction can't be done on a tight schedule.

Architecture, because it is so dependent on process, provides an excellent illustration of how questioning traditional professional practice, or "hacking" it, as Michael Murphy says, is the most effective way to change its impact. The same principles apply to any profession and any issue: if the process is the strategy, the most effective path to change an outcome is to interrogate and modify the process that leads to it.

Although this story is about how one firm is revealing and reinventing the hidden power dynamics of architecture in order to create social value, every industry has its silent, yet inviolate, set of rules in need of breaking. Integrating the principles and process of social design provides the way.

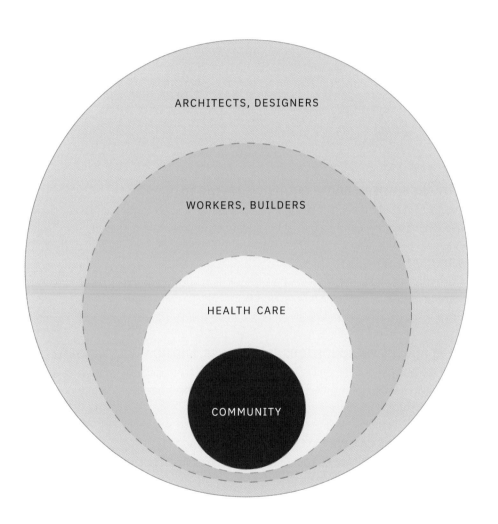

HOW MASS DESIGN GROUP ANSWERED THE SOCIAL DESIGN PROCESS QUESTIONS

WHY ARE WE HERE, AND WHAT ARE WE TRYING TO DO?
Design built environments that support social justice and contribute to the well-being of entire communities while raising the standards for beauty and function.

WHAT'S THE CONTEXT?
Places of crisis and extreme need, where inequities in health care and income create vulnerability. Residents of the built environments, and the entire communities around them, are key stakeholders, in addition to designers, builders, funders, and governments.

WHAT ARE THE PRECONDITIONS FOR SUCCESS, AND HOW WILL WE KNOW IT?
Both the process and the end result will benefit the communities in which they are built. Jobs will be created, well-being improved, and skills advanced locally while the environmental footprint is reduced.

WHAT ACTIONS CAN WE TAKE TO GET THERE?
Question everything. Put the community's well-being first. Hack the process of creating a built environment.

DOES IT WORK?
Measure not in awards or financial return but in outcomes for the people for whom it is intended.

CHAPTER 14

Getting from
There to Here

IT'S ABUNDANTLY CLEAR THAT IN THEIR CURRENT STATE, our society and our relationships with each other need a redesign. Social design offers a process for leading
that change. It contradicts the prevalent assumption that the burden of reimagining
and reinventing our future is on someone else's shoulders, that the conditions that
affect us all can be entrusted only to those who call themselves experts.

The real and ultimate benefit of social design is that it gives those who practice
it an awareness of the agency we all have to create something different from what
we know. This is the basis of hope. Designers are, and have always been, essentially
hopeful people because they know that every day is an opportunity to wake up and invent something new, to see challenges in a different way, to reframe problems so they
can be solved. This awareness of the resourcefulness we all possess, if we will learn
to use it, provides internal strength and confidence. Picasso said that "the artist goes
through states of emptiness and fullness, and that is all there is to the mystery of art."
It is this fullness, the sense of possibility, that we all need and that social design provides for companies and communities. In social design, it is not the lone individual's

potential but the potential of everyone. Not independently and in ways that compete but as the creative, collaborative beings we are capable of being.

IF SOCIAL DESIGN MAKES SO MUCH SENSE, WHY ISN'T EVERYONE DOING IT?

The principles in the system presented here can seem so familiar and practical that we feel as if we know them all already. "Well, of course, the people most affected by whatever is being designed should have a voice in what it is," one might think. "They probably do know what would work for them better than an outsider does." And "Of course, the only certain way to ensure that a big, expensive innovation works for users is to get their feedback along the way and make decisions based on evidence rather than trying to guess in advance how people will react."

However practical and obvious they sound, when applied in practice these principles are revolutionary for people with ingrained habits (all of us). They shake the ground under entrenched power structures that are the source of comfort for some and oppression for others. When the time comes to act on these principles instead of only professing them, the established pecking order is threatened. When ideas come not only from the top but from everywhere, contribution, and therefore value, is redefined. When inquiry is favored over fast decisions, those accustomed to being decision makers, the experts who have made their reputations with ready answers, are required to change their game. It is a challenge for those with a need to be the "smartest person in the room" to be gratified by making the whole room smarter. Respected experts toil their whole lives to earn the position they hold as the person who inevitably knows what should be done. People who need to know their next ten steps in advance don't like to step off the edge of faux certainty. Managers who demand fast and conclusive answers from their subordinates don't want to hear about the benefits of not knowing.

Even when organizations try to adopt the principles of social design, there are forces at work to prevent the old power dynamics and habits from changing. Consultancies, filled with experts who survive by appearing to know more than the people who hire them, profit from complicating common processes until they look like intellectual property. People in marketing or innovation departments or those who work in the field of development rightly say they already know everything there is to know about their customers and end users. They believe they can and should continue to speak for them. And those more at ease with transactions than relationships often simply don't understand what all the fuss is about.

The social design process often uncovers challenges different from those assumed to be there. It takes enormous courage to march into uncharted territory and toward that kind of vulnerability. It's a lot like remodeling an old house. Once the guts are uncovered, surprises emerge that need to be addressed whether they were written into the plans or not. Whereas we know this about old houses—that to make them livable, those hidden issues need to be discovered and resolved—it doesn't automatically carry over into our work with cultures. And whereas it's obvious that fixing a house's problems when they are found is more efficient than putting them off for a later date, it's not as easy to explain why this messy process of including the people affected by whatever we're building together is more efficient than trying to avoid its messiness. It can be difficult to see, until you see it, that time devoted to the minutiae of "other people's problems" is the best way to get to massive scale.

Mutually beneficial change takes a long time, something we don't know how to deal with in the twenty-first century. The days of lone heroes and quick fixes are over, and they never were what we hoped they would be. Problems are too complex to fix quickly, too big for us to fix alone. The inbox erupts with invitations to meet-ups, conversations, two-day conferences, webinars and courses promising to provide the kind of wisdom it takes years to earn. Time is not the appropriate metric for anything but races and three-minute eggs, though we have allowed it to become the metronome of our modern lives: quarterly earnings, overnight successes, two-day workweeks, and instant mashed potatoes.

Creating has its own rhythms—of doing and watching, asking and synthesizing. And not all time is equal; some is for waiting, some for acting. If we measure progress rather than time, it will connect us more deeply to the systems we touch, teach us to honor the rules of nature. It will make us aware of the resources we use, the quality and beauty of what we produce. It will give us a healthy mistrust of shortcuts and quick fixes.

TO THE QUESTION OF WHERE TO BEGIN

As the bicycle salesman quoted at the beginning of this book said, look at where you want to go, not at what's in your way. First, imagine the new reality you and your collaborators want to create. Define it in concrete terms, not abstract ones. Lofty is fine, but make it actionable, and make sure it's described specifically enough that you will recognize it when you get there. This takes work, and it is the single most important act in the entire process. Most people think they are being concrete when they're not, either because they think what's in their head is conveyed in words that don't communicate to others what they are thinking or because it's hard to get concrete about an image of the future. Next, draw a map of that new reality with all the systems and people it touches, like the diagrams included in each of the stories presented here. Then determine all the things that need to happen for you to get there, and be prepared to rethink and revise constantly on the basis of real-time evidence along the way. These few steps alone will get you started on a journey far different from the one that formed our current civilization. And, though first prize in an intergalactic design competition may be something you have your eye on, don't make that your goal. It's an unintended consequence of getting everything else right along the way.

Every social designer included here is a leader. They are inventors, entrepreneurs, creators, writers, scientists, and businesspeople. Most relevant, they are leaders who listen to other people and learn from them, who can articulate a vision in a way that people see themselves in it, and who can facilitate a process that moves beyond invention or novelty to fulfill a higher purpose. Leaders are needed now—people who will step up and do it. I hope that by now, it is evident that this can be you.

Some Things Worth Reading

Baldwin, James, Richard Wright, and Norman Mailer. *Nobody Knows My Name.* Reissue ed. New York: Vintage Books, 1992.

Diamond, Jared M. *Guns, Germs, and Steel: The Fates of Human Societies.* New York: W. W. Norton, 1999.

Easterly, William. *The Tyranny of Experts: Economists, Dictators, and the Forgotten Rights of the Poor.* New York: Basic Books, 2014.

Frank, Robert H. "A Champion of Plain English." *New York Times,* January 8, 2011. Accessed July 20, 2016. www.nytimes.com/2011/01/09/business/09view.html?_r=1.

Fritz, Robert. *Creating: A Practical Guide to the Creative Process and How to Use It to Create* Anything—a Work of Art, a Relationship, a Career, or a Better Life. New York: Ballantine Books, 1993.

Gopnik, Adam. *Angels and Ages: A Short Book about Darwin, Lincoln, and Modern Life.* New York: Vintage Books, 2010.

Hawken, Paul. *Blessed Unrest: How the Largest Social Movement in History Is Restoring Grace, Justice, and Beauty to the World*. New York: Penguin Books, 2008.

Kolbert, Elizabeth. "Unnatural Selection: What Will It Take to Save the World's Reefs and Forests?" *New Yorker*, April 8, 2016. Accessed July 1, 2017. www.newyorker.com/magazine/2016/04/18/a-radical-attempt-to-save-the-reefs-and-forests.

Lakoff, George. *Don't Think of an Elephant! Know Your Values and Frame the Debate: The Essential Guide for Progressives*. White River Junction, VT: Chelsea Green, 2005.

McDonough, William, and Michael Braungart. *Cradle to Cradle: Remaking the Way We Make Things*. New York: North Point Press, 2002.

Orr, David W. *Earth in Mind: On Education, Environment, and the Human Prospect*. Washington, DC: Island Press, 2004.

Orwell, George. *Politics and the English Language and Other Essays*. [Garsington, UK?]: Benediction Classics, 2010.

Papanek, Victor. *Design for the Real World: Human Ecology and Social Change*. 2nd rev. ed. Chicago: Chicago Review Press, 2005.

Polak, Paul. *Out of Poverty: What Works When Traditional Approaches Fail*. San Francisco: Berrett-Koehler, 2009.

Ueland, Brenda. *If You Want to Write: A Book about Art, Independence, and Spirit*. [United States]: BN Publishing, 2010.

Wheatley, Margaret J. *Leadership and the New Science: Discovering Order in a Chaotic World*. 3rd ed. San Francisco: Berrett-Koehler, 2006.

Acknowledgments

COUNTLESS PEOPLE HAVE TAUGHT AND INSPIRED ME. A few have changed my life. Paul Polak set an example for a way to live that redrew the boundaries I and others had drawn around me. When they were erased, he patiently talked me through the process of inventing a new way to be. Jaimie Cloud gave me hope in the form of all the writers and thinkers who put earthly wisdom into words, David Orr among them. PopTech and its Social Innovation Fellows gave me the opportunity to work with and learn from people who invent new models for business and society every day. Leetha Filderman has been a cherished partner on that PopTech journey. Cheryl Kiser, my sister from another mother, gives me spiritual kinship and a priceless partnership in thinking about what's possible. Kenny Fries and Reiko Rizzuto taught me how to write. Richard Wilde led me into teaching and showed me how a mensch does it. David Rhodes and the School of Visual Arts had the principles and conviction to start something.

Deep thanks to all the extraordinary leaders profiled in this book, for doing what they do. And to their teams, for their patient assistance: Jon Khoo from Interface, Colleen Kelly from Brown's Super Stores, Kari Bonaro from Buffalo Niagara Medical Campus, Chiara Brambilla from Aquafil, Kira Hughes from Gates Coral Lab, David Mistretta and Kareya Saleh from MASS Design Group.

Thanks to the Rockefeller Foundation and its Bellagio Fellows Program, for giving me space and place to finish the manuscript, and to Pilar Palaciá and my fellow Fellows for their gentle support.

I am grateful to every one of my many extraordinary women friends, for being loving, fierce, and funny. To my sister, Lynn, for her heroism as a caregiver. To the Design for Social Innovation (DSI) faculty for creating a groundbreaking graduate program, for being in it together, and for loving the students: Siri Betts-Sonstegard, Maggie Breslin, Mattie Brice, Asi Burak, Jaimie Cloud, Archie Lee Coates IV, Alison Cornyn, Pat Dandonoli, Hannah du Plessis, Jane Englebardt, Nicholas Fortugno, Jeffrey Franklin, Lee-Sean Huang, Natasha Kanagat, Julie Kennedy, Anne LaFonde, Amanda Makulec, Caroline McAndrews, Aurelia Moser, Miya Osaki, Despina Papadopoulos, Tina Park, Benedetta Piantella, Karen Proctor, Natalia Radywyl, Marc Rettig, Gabriel Schuster, Lina Srivastava, and Maya Weinstein. Thanks to every student in the program for every day, and every class, even at your most challenging, and thanks especially to my dear Pragya Mahendru for her help with this book. Thanks to my editor, Courtney Lix, for seeing the vision and getting it on paper. Thanks to Kyle Reis for connecting me to Island Press and offering so many kinds of support along the way. To Ray for being himself, always. And to my husband, Gary—everything that can be said is a cliché, and every day together is priceless beyond words.

Notes Notes

Chapter 1
The Answer to Everything

1. David W. Orr, *Earth in Mind: On Education, Environment, and the Human Prospect* (Washington, DC: Island Press, 2004; first published 1994).
2. Paul Hawken, *Blessed Unrest: How the Largest Social Movement in History Is Restoring Grace, Justice, and Beauty to the World* (New York: Penguin Books, 2008).
3. For example, see Ecovative Design, Green Island, New York, www.ecovativedesign.com/.
4. The United Nations, the United Nations International Children's Emergency Fund, the U.S. Agency for International Development, and the Department for International Development (United Kingdom), respectively.

Chapter 2
Seeing Edges and Patterns, Scoping and Framing

1. Attributed to R. Buckminster Fuller, as reported by one of his former colleagues.
2. Eric Ries, *The Lean Startup: How Today's Entrepreneurs Use Continuous Innovation to Create Radically Successful Businesses* (New York: Currency, 2011).
3. William Safire, "The New Groupthink," *New York Times*, July 14, 2004, accessed January 6, 2018, www.nytimes.com/2004/07/14/opinion/the-new-groupthink.html.

Chapter 3
Past as Prologue

1. R. Buckminster Fuller and Kiyoshi Kuromiya, *Cosmography: A Posthumous Scenario for the Future of Humanity* (New York: Macmillan, 1992), p. 8.

2. Victor Papanek, *Design for the Real World: Human Ecology and Social Change*, 2nd rev. ed. (Chicago: Chicago Review Press, 2005; first published 1984 by Academy Chicago Publishers).

3. "*Design for the Real World: Human Ecology and Social Change* (1971) by Victor Papanek (1923–1998)," *Design Thinking @ Haas* (blog), April 30, 2012, https://divergentmba.wordpress.com/2012/04/29/design-for-the-real-world-human-ecology-and-social-change-1971-by-victor-papanek-1923-1998-10/.

4. William McDonough and Michael Braungart, *Cradle to Cradle: Remaking the Way We Make Things* (New York: North Point Press, 2002).

5. *Design for the Other 90%* (2007 exhibition at Cooper Hewitt, National Design Museum), accessed July 3, 2017, http://archive.cooperhewitt.org/other90/other90.cooperhewitt.org/index.html.

Chapter 4
Mastering the System

1. Jacob Morgan, "Why the Millions We Spend on Employee Engagement Buy Us So Little," *Harvard Business Review*, March 10, 2017, https://hbr.org/2017/03/why-the-millions-we-spend-on-employee-engagement-buy-us-so-little.

2. William Easterly, *The Tyranny of Experts: Economists, Dictators, and the Forgotten Rights of the Poor* (New York: Basic Books, 2014).

3. Robert Fritz, *Creating: A Practical Guide to the Creative Process and How to Use It to Create* Anything—*a Work of Art, a Relationship, a Career, or a Better Life* (New York: Ballantine Books, 1993).

4. John Sheesley, "Destroying the Planet One iPhone at a Time," TechRepublic, July 23, 2008, www.techrepublic.com/blog/decision-central/destroying-the-planet-one-iphone-at-a-time/.

5. Originally posted in the online magazine *Impact Design Hub*, https://impactdesignhub.org/2016/03/09/unsteady-ground-impact-designers-on-the-new-age-of-uncertainty/ (site discontinued).

6. Jared M. Diamond, *Guns, Germs, and Steel: The Fates of Human Societies* (New York: W. W. Norton, 1999).

7. Google Search results for "What Are Soft Skills," accessed July 15, 2017, www.google.com/search?q=what+are+soft+skills&ie=utf-8&oe=utf-8.

Chapter 6
Ruth Gates: Mixing Science and Social Design to Address Climate Change

1. University of Hawai'i at Mānoa, Department of Biology, "Ruth Gates: Research Interests," accessed September 30, 2017, https://manoa.hawaii.edu/biology /people/ruth-gates.

Chapter 7
The Salvage Supperclub: Navigating with Feedback Loops

1. Dana Gunders, Natural Resources Defense Council, "Wasted: How America Is Losing up to 40 Percent of Its Food from Farm to Fork to Landfill," NRDC Issue Paper IP:12-06-B, August 2012, www.nrdc.org/sites/default/files/wasted-food-IP.pdf, p. 1.
2. Jay Winsten, "The Designated Driver Campaign: Why It Worked," *Huffington Post*, March 18, 2010, www.huffingtonpost.com/jay-winston/designated-driver -campaig_b_405249.html.

Chapter 8
Interface Net-Works: Creating New Models and Solving Problems along the Way

1. Global Alliance for Incinerator Alternatives (GAIA) and Changing Markets, "Swept Under the Carpet: Exposing the Greenwash of the U.S. Carpet Industry," www.no-burn .org/wp-content/uploads/SWEPT-UNDER-THE-CARPET_high-res-DECEMBER-2016 .pdf. The executive summary (p. 4) states, "In 2014, the carpet industry in the United States (U.S.) produced 11.7 billion square feet of carpet and rugs."
2. Katherine Martinko, "America's Carpet Industry Needs Cleaning Up," TreeHugger, March 29, 2017, accessed October 18, 2017, www.treehugger.com/corporate -responsibility/americas-carpet-industry-environmental-disaster.html.
3. Paul Hawken, *The Ecology of Commerce: A Declaration of Sustainability*, rev. ed. (New York: Harper Business, 2010).
4. Mikhail Davis, "20 Years Later, Interface Looks Back on Ray Anderson's Legacy," GreenBiz, September 3, 2014, accessed October 22, 2017, www.greenbiz.com /blog/2014/09/03/20-years-later-interface-looks-back-ray-andersons-legacy.
5. Ray C. Anderson and Robin White, *Confessions of a Radical Industrialist: Profits, People, Purpose—Doing Business by Respecting the Earth* (New York: St. Martin's Press, 2009).
6. Niall Smith, "Interview: Miriam Turner, InterfaceFLOR," *Guardian*, August 24, 2011, www.theguardian.com/social-enterprise-network/2011/aug/24/qa-on-purpose -associate-interfaceflor.

Chapter 9
Erik Hersman: Tapping the Power of Limits

1. Ken Banks, ed., *The Rise of the Reluctant Innovator: When Problems Find People, Amazing Things Can Happen* (London: London Publishing Partnership, 2013), Kindle edition, Kindle location 626–633.

Chapter 10
Paul Polak: The Story Is in the Context

1. World Bank, "Poverty: Overview," accessed June 3, 2017, www.worldbank.org/en /topic/poverty/overview.
2. Jerry cans are heavy-duty containers for liquids, originally made from pressed steel and developed for military use in the 1930s. They typically hold twenty liters.
3. From Polak's book *The Business Solution to Poverty*: "The emerging economies of the Global South, not even counting China and Russia, collectively generate $12 trillion, or nearly one-fifth (18 percent) of the world's total economic output. . . . And every year, according to the *Financial Times*, approximately $1 trillion more is invested in emerging economies." Paul Polak and Mal Warwick, *The Business Solution to Poverty: Designing Products and Services for Three Billion New Customers* (San Francisco: Berrett-Koehler, 2013), pp. 4, 62.
4. This is my own version, expanded by observation of Paul Polak. You can see his version here: http://socialcapitalmarkets.net/2009/11/interview-with-paul-polak -over-17-million-customers-served/.
5. Polak tells the story of a Bangladeshi version of a Bollywood film in which a young couple could not marry because the woman's father couldn't afford a dowry, leading to a near-suicide averted only when a friend recommended a treadle pump, leading to a successful cash crop harvest, leading to a dowry, a marriage, and a happily-ever-after. The film was promoted and screened in villages on the side of a truck, powered by a generator and accompanied by a paid demonstrator of how easy the treadle pump is to operate.

Chapter 11
The Buffalo Niagara Medical Campus: Using Networks to Create a New Future for a City

1. David W. Chen, "Border War over the Peace Bridge," *New York Times*, April 27, 1999, www.nytimes.com/1999/04/27/nyregion/border-war-over-the-peace-bridge.html.

Chapter 12
Sisi ni Amani: Communicating the Way to Nonviolence

1. Sasha Chanoff, "Tribal Hatred Didn't Cause Violence in Kenya," *Boston Globe*, January 19, 2008, accessed November 18, 2017, http://archive.boston.com /bostonglobe/editorial_opinion/oped/articles/2008/01/19/tribal_hatred_didnt _cause_violence_in_kenya/.

2. Patrick Meier, "How Crisis Mapping Saved Lives in Haiti," National Geographic Society blogs, July 2, 2012, https://newswatch.nationalgeographic.org/2012/07/02 /crisis-mapping-haiti/.

3. Nona Lambert and Sabina Carlson, "The Virtual Field: Remote Crisis Mapping of the Haitian Earthquake," *Praxis: The Fletcher Journal of Human Security* 25 (2010): 87–92 (quotation p. 87), http://fletcher.tufts.edu/Praxis/Archives/~/media /F9A582962046417F9E01077A30F66EC5.pdf.

4. Human Rights Watch, "Ballots to Bullets: Organized Political Violence and Kenya's Crisis of Governance," March 16, 2008, www.hrw.org/report/2008/03/16/ballots -bullets/organized-political-violence-and-kenyas-crisis-governance.

5. Seema Shah and Rachel Brown, "Programming for Peace: Sisi Ni Amani Kenya and the 2013 Elections," CGCS Occasional Paper Series on ICTs, Statebuilding, and Peacebuilding in Africa, No. 3 (Philadelphia: University of Pennsylvania, Annenberg School for Communication, Center for Global Communications Studies, December 2014), www.global.asc.upenn.edu/app/uploads/2014/12/SisiNiAmaniReport.pdf.

Chapter 13
MASS Design Group: Process Is Strategy

1. MASS Design Group, "The Butaro District Hospital," https://massdesigngroup.org /work/design/butaro-district-hospital.

CHERYL HELLER has a history of building new capacities within organizations that expand their reach and make them more resilient. She is the Founding Chair of the first MFA program in Design for Social Innovation at SVA, with alums now working as change leaders in industry, government and the social sector. She is the founder of the design consultancy CommonWise and of the Measured Lab, which she created in 2017 to investigate the impact of social design on human health. She founded the first design department in a major advertising agency and as a strategist, has helped grow businesses from small regional enterprises to multi-billion global market leaders, launched category-redefining divisions and products, reinvigorated moribund cultures, and designed strategies for hundreds of successful entrepreneurs. She has taught creativity to leaders and organizations around the world. Heller is a recipient of the prestigious AIGA Medal for her contribution to the field of design and was recently recognized by the Rockefeller Foundation with a Bellagio Fellowship.

Her clients have included Ford Motor Company, American Express, Reebok, Mariott International, MeadWestvaco, StoraEnso, the Arnhold Institute for Global Health, Medtronic, Mars Corporation, Discovery Networks International, Herman Miller, Bayer Corporation, Seventh Generation, L'Oreal, Elle Magazine, Harper's Bazaar, The World Wildlife Fund, Ford Foundation, Lumina Foundation, The Graduate Network and the Girl Scouts of America.

Heller is the former Board Chair of PopTech, and a Senior Fellow at the Babson Social Innovation Lab. She created the Ideas that Matter program for Sappi in 1999, which has since given over $14 million to designers working for the public good, and partnered with Paul Polak and the Cooper Hewitt National Design Museum to create the exhibit, "Design for the Other 90%." She is currently working on a Ph.D at RMIT University in Melbourne.